The New
Global Leaders

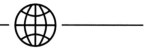

The New Global Leaders

Richard Branson, Percy Barnevik, and David Simon

Manfred F. R. Kets de Vries
with Elizabeth Florent-Treacy

Jossey-Bass Publishers
San Francisco

Copyright © 1999 by Jossey-Bass Inc., Publishers, 350 Sansome Street, San Francisco, California 94104.

Jossey-Bass books and products are available through most bookstores. To contact Jossey-Bass directly, call (888) 378-2537, fax to (800) 605-2665, or visit our website at www.josseybass.com.

Substantial discounts on bulk quantities of Jossey-Bass books are available to corporations, professional associations, and other organizations. For details and discount information, contact the special sales department at Jossey-Bass.

Library of Congress Cataloging-in-Publication Data

Kets de Vries, Manfred F. R.
   The new global leaders: Richard Branson, Percy Barnevik, and David Simon/
   Manfred F. R. Kets de Vries with Elizabeth Florent-Treacy.—1st ed.
      p. cm.
   Includes bibliographical references and index.
      ISBN 0-7879-4657-5 (acid-free paper)
   1. International business enterprises—Management—Case studies. 2. Organizational change—Case studies. 3. Richard Branson. 4. Virgin Group. 5. Barnevik, Percy. 6. British Petroleum Company. 7. David Simon. 8. ABB Asea Brown Boveri Ltd. I. Florent-Treacy, Elizabeth, 1960 II. Title.
HD62.4 .K484 1999
658'.049—dc21   98-51225

Contents

To Oriane, wise-before-the-events
M. K. de V.

Aux îlots qui me donnent le courage de naviguer au large
E. F.-T.

Acknowledgments

The poet John Donne wrote, "No man is an island, entire of itself; every man is a piece of a continent." This is certainly true when it comes to writing a book. We consider ourselves fortunate to be part of a large group of professional and very patient colleagues. We could not have undertaken this project without the help and support of INSEAD's R&D department—in particular Landis Gabel and the always good-natured Alison James—and without the long-term encouragement of the former and present deans of INSEAD, Ludo Van der Heyden and Antonio Borges. We would also like to acknowledge and thank those who did important work in developing the material in this book. Robert Dick coauthored the case study on Richard Branson. For Part Two, on Percy Barnevik, the case coauthor was Raafat Morcos; thorough (and bilingual) background research and interviews were done by Christopher Grahn, Casten von Otter, and Peter Gullander; Elisabet Engellau assisted with the Barnevik interview.

Last, but far from least, we extend our appreciation and thanks to the four men without whom this book would not exist: Richard Branson, Percy Barnevik, Sir David Simon, and John Browne.

There are several people who worked tirelessly behind the scenes to meld a pile of disparate texts into this real book. Sally Simmons was an intrepid winnower, instrumental in shaping the book. She also contributed the research and writing that links the case studies and interviews together. We thank her for her hard work. We benefited greatly from the pragmatic and professional work of our virtual editor from another continent, Kathy Reigstad. Sheila Loxham, who wisely kept her fingers out of the pie, was invaluable as always for her strategic support, good humor in the face of numerous snafus, and genuine Irish coffees. And we certainly would be remiss if we didn't acknowledge the very encouraging support of our editor at Jossey-Bass, Cedric Crocker.

Finally, we would like to thank friends and family who help pull us through the discouraging times. In one sense, Donne was wrong: these people are like sunny private islands in a stormy sea, to whom we turn for courage, rest, or just a breath of fresh air. Elizabeth Florent-Treacy would like to express her deep gratitude to Frédéric, Robin, and Luc. Manfred Kets de Vries would like to single out his brother, Florian.

Fontainebleau, France
June 1998

MANFRED KETS DE VRIES
ELIZABETH FLORENT-TREACY

Preface:
Role Models for Tomorrow

Anyone scanning the front pages of the major business journals over the past few years probably has the impression that being an executive in a global corporation is like crossing a minefield. Dangers abound. Although we read far more bad news than good— articles about the fallout of mergers and acquisitions, about global alliances that are torn apart, about expatriate assignments that end unsuccessfully—there are international business *success* stories as well; there are exceptions to the rule. Three global leaders stand out among those success stories because they have struggled—and managed—to create world-class organizations. In their quest for answers to questions concerning appropriate leadership styles, they are role models for the new global organization.

Richard Branson (founder and head of the Virgin Group), Percy Barnevik (mastermind behind the merger of ASEA and Brown Boveri to form ABB), and David Simon (former CEO of British Petroleum) all looked for ways to create a greater sense of purpose for their employees while putting in place the structure necessary for a global organization. In their own search for meaning, these leaders created a vision that clarifies what the organization stands for, highlights the organization's purpose, and outlines the values and beliefs that define the organization's corporate culture. In addition, they specified objectives and strategies to make that vision reality.

We see Virgin, ABB, and BP as examples of a new organizational paradigm. The leaders of these global corporations show that they have the skill not only to design a multicultural strategy but also—and perhaps more important—to mobilize their people. The international acumen that Branson, Barnevik, and Simon possess enables them to keep their organizations at the forefront in global markets. At the same time, these leaders have created world-class firms based on a new kind of psychological contract; they have sustained change and innovation in their organizations without forfeiting the respect and loyalty of their subordinates.

How do these men see the changed relationship between leaders and their constituencies? How do they make the process work in a global organization? Though their corporations have undergone different kinds of cultural change—ABB in a merger, BP in a restructuring process, and Virgin in a continuous remix of its companies—we can see strong similarities in how each of the three developed an adaptive learning culture that fosters stability in a context of innovation. It is their strong qualities as global leaders, combined with their attention to people's search for meaning in their work, that make these three CEOs stand out.

The values and beliefs that drive Barnevik, Branson, and Simon are an integral part of their individual vision, motivating them to spread their message with passion and conviction. In these men, we see leaders who know how to create enthusiasm and commitment that inspire others. We see leaders who, recognizing the importance of their roles as change-agent, cheerleader, coach, teacher, mentor, and integrator, change the way their people work by helping them change their attitude toward work. We see leaders who instill in their employees a kind of pride that goes beyond the numbers game. Recognizing the importance of contributing to society, they foster corporate values that answer some basic human needs—notably, identity and meaning—but with a crucial difference: their organizations work through team effort, not patriarchal hierarchy. Through the collective efforts of the men and women who make up their organizations, these leaders hope that their companies are perceived as changing the world positively.

THE GLOBAL ORGANIZATION: A CHANGE IN PARADIGM

As we cannot fail to be aware, life in modern organizations is no longer what it was for our parents' generation. The world has changed dramatically. These days, being internationally competitive is the name of the game. With the dissolution of international trade barriers and the evolution of a new global economy, many companies have gone through a continuum of transition from being international (stressing an export-import orientation), to being multinational (having major operations abroad that are concentrated on specific, relatively protected markets), to being global (looking at the entire world as a market). The new, total global economy has come of age.

No longer can any of us survive in splendid isolation. We are all part of the same complex, increasingly interlinked world. The global interconnectedness made possible—no, *mandated*—by advances in technology and communication challenges every organization with the perils of discontinuity. To meet those challenges, corporate leaders are working to develop new organizational forms. These new types of companies—some already taking shape—have a global perspective, with a number of centralized functions, accompanied by decentralized authority for country or regional management. These new global corporations—organizations that have direct and indirect affiliations worldwide through manufacturing, sourcing, distribution, marketing, and sales facilities—are the models of the future. Such organizations need to think in global strategic terms; with their assets and risks deployed around the world, they cannot be overly biased by the national perspective of the headquarters location. And because their operations link groups of global business managers, country or regional managers, and worldwide functional managers, they recruit management talent not locally but from around the world.

After enjoying a long period of stability, steady growth, and largely domestic competition after World War II until well into the 1980s, organizations in recent years have been forced by rapidly changing international markets and the global economy to adopt the new corporate profile—that is, to become *global* organizations—or go under. The emerging web of relationships resulting from this corporate evolution brings about global-scale efficiency and competitiveness. However, worldwide benchmarking also leads to restructuring, downsizing, and increasing dependence on temporary workers—trends that have (and will continue to have) a tremendous impact on organizations and their people.

The communication and information revolution, demographic shifts in population, and major political and economic changes in

Eastern Europe and Asia necessitate adaptation to an entirely new (and rather unpredictable) environment. The opening of markets in China and the former Soviet Union provides opportunities that executives in many organizations could not and cannot afford to miss. Continuing European integration offers a further challenge, stretching people's adaptive capabilities. As a result of all these factors, decision making, although increasingly complex, must occur at a much faster pace than it used to, putting extreme pressure on each individual's capability to process information.

All these changes in the global economy are transforming not only organizations themselves but also the relationship between people and their organizations. In other words, the essential organizational paradigm is evolving.

In the new global corporation, hierarchical structures, with their many well-defined layers of management and seniority, cede their place to flat, boundaryless networks. Functional structures give way to organizations favoring a process orientation. Technological innovation continues to put its stamp on organizations, but the organization of the future will be increasingly customer-driven, as service expectations continue to grow. Whereas capital was once a company's scarcest and most valued resource, knowledge has become the new organization's most critical asset.

This new global world also makes the homegrown, up-through-the-ranks, insular CEO of the past less relevant. A recent *Wall Street Journal* article predicted that by the turn of the century, organizations will choose leaders according to their ability to deal with international competition, globalization of markets, the spread of technology, demographic shifts, and the speed of overall change. With ever more business battles taking place across borders, executives need to be knowledgeable about foreign markets and international competition. As organizations go through a global "revolution," they require the leadership of a significantly different kind of CEO.

Unfortunately, the organizational revolution demanded by the global marketplace must occur faster than executive attitudes typically evolve. Within virtually a single generation, our comfortable existence in a familiar home culture has been shaken by an awareness that we cannot escape being part of this global, interconnected environment. The inward-looking, parochial attitude that served us well for decades is now extremely costly. Leaders who hold on to this attitude set up their organizations to become diminished players in the global market. To survive in today's interconnected world, the global executive needs a different mind-set.

THE NEW GLOBAL EXECUTIVE

Many of the leading CEOs of the postwar era were individuals with a financial or technical background and a military mentality—people used to giving orders and having them obeyed. Alfred Sloan of General Motors is a good example of this type of leader. Under his direction, GM became the quintessential "modern" corporation. In the somewhat insular world of Sloan's postwar chairmanship, relational skills and international experience were not considered essential competencies.

Executives of the next century, however, will have quite a different competency set—one geared toward tackling intensifying worldwide competition. Effective executives in the new corporation are likely to have a humanities or engineering degree and an MBA. They will have worked in many of the organization's foreign subsidiaries. These new executives are going to be team players, used to working in high-level management teams with people of diverse cultural backgrounds. Because a collegial leadership style is more acceptable than an autocratic approach for the global organization of tomorrow, leaders of the future cultivate an authoritative rather than authoritarian way of dealing with people. Position, status, and seniority are of less importance to corporations hiring and promoting executives than proven competence in dealing with a world of rapid, continuous change.

"Soft"—that is, relational—skills are essential for the new global executive. Technical expertise alone is no longer adequate. To be effective in the global economy, executives need to possess strategic awareness of, and deep interest in, the socioeconomic and political scene of the countries in which they operate. To understand what is happening in the world around them, these global executives also need to be talented at both verbal and nonverbal communication. Leaders at the helm of the corporations of the future will need the capacity to step out of their own comfort zone and adapt to other realities. The ability to speak more than one language well is a sign of that capacity.

Because ethnocentricity and dogmatism are not acceptable attitudes in the emerging global corporation, global executives possess cross-cultural empathy; in other words, they are able to relate to individuals from diverse backgrounds. Moreover, they have a strong sense of self—and of their own cultural biases. Building on that foundation, they acquire rich knowledge of a culture other than their own to gain a sense of perspective. Those executives who are effective in the new global economy will be those who recognize that diversity in national outlook is the name of the game. They are nonjudgmental, acknowledging and valuing people's differences. However, they also appreciate what is common among various nationalities, remaining open to mental borders as much as national ones. If this mind-set, this valuing of diversity in culture and outlook, is to permeate the organization, it must emanate from the top. From the CEO down, leaders have to set the example.

Leaders of the future will also be curious, a quality that helps them adapt to foreign environments. They possess a sense of adventure, a positive outlook toward life. They are willing to take risks; they are resilient, unwilling to give up even when the chips are down; and they exhibit a willingness to learn and adapt, to acquire new patterns of behavior and attitudes. They have a high tolerance for frustration and a flexible outlook toward people and events; they can live comfortably with considerable ambiguity.

CEOs of world-class organizations draw on these softer skills to accomplish four main tasks:

1. Articulating a compelling strategy with a multicountry, multi-environment, and multifunctional perspective that connects employees on a global scale
2. Designing the organization so that appropriate structures are in place to align the behavior of employees
3. Inculcating a global mentality in the ranks—that is, instilling values that act as a sort of glue between the national cultures represented in the organization

4. Mobilizing and motivating people to actualize their specific vision of the future

As experienced CEOs have discovered—contrary to the glorious role assigned to strategy making in textbooks and classrooms—most of the real work of leadership concerns *process;* it involves inspiring, motivating, and giving feedback to one's people wherever they are on the globe. It is this fourth task of leadership that poses the greatest challenge to the global leader. David Whitwam, CEO of Whirlpool, is quoted as saying that for a company to become a truly global enterprise, employees have to change how they think and act, taking on progressively more responsibility and initiative until the company behaves globally in all of its parts.

Executives in the global corporation have to accept that the unstated psychological contract between individual and organization is in flux. The relationship between leader and led is not what it used to be. The consequent climate of uncertainty arouses workers' dependency needs, resulting in a desire for containment of anxiety through concerned leadership. This state of affairs creates a paradox, however. Executives in this global world are expected by those who pay them to have a high tolerance for ambiguity, but at the same time, they are expected by those who report to them to create a secure "holding environment" that reduces the anxiety of ambiguity! In other words, leaders are asked to be beacons of certitude in a highly uncertain world.

A NEW PSYCHOLOGICAL CONTRACT

Unfortunately, given the vicissitudes of the new global environment, the majority of executives in large organizations are asked to tolerate more ambiguity than they are comfortable with. Because organizations are no longer the haven of security that they once were, people who count on organizations to take care of them for the long term—and contain anxiety about the future—are bound to be disappointed. The traditional company person—that deeply loyal individual who enjoyed a sense of security and who confidently expected annual salary increases and a growing pension in return for loyalty—has become an endangered species in this age of restructuring and reengineering. The safety net once provided by the large corporation has all but disappeared. Because of this changing psychological contract, stress disorders are on the rise; the mental health of many executives and employees is affected.

As might be expected, these changes in organizational relationships lead to increased cynicism and decreased morale. Looking ahead to an uncertain future after many years of loyal service to their company, many long-term employees feel betrayed. The popularity of the *Dilbert* cartoons, which highlight the difference between organizational rhetoric and reality, is symptomatic of the changing psychological contract. Like Dilbert, many of today's corporate people, nostalgic for the sense of community they once knew in the workplace, feel imprisoned in their cubicles. They respond by sleepwalking through their corporate environment, saving whatever creative ideas they have for life outside the corporation.

But a jaundiced outlook toward corporate life is not a necessity. Not *all* senior executives are blind to their employees' needs. Some leaders in this new global world know how to create "good-enough" containment. They know how to get the best out of their people, they understand the limits of ambiguity, and they can make work meaningful. Given these traits, they are able to get extraordinary results out of ordinary people.

THE IMPORTANCE OF WORK IN THE HUMAN EXPERIENCE

This brings us to the question of what makes work meaningful—why we work and what work means to us. As a way of establishing identity and maintaining self-esteem, work has always been an anchor of psychological well-being. Freud's definition of mental health as *lieben und arbeiten* (to love and to work) still rings true. Organizations are arenas in which we cope with the stresses and strains of daily life and act out the script of our inner theater. Work defines—either positively or negatively—our feelings of effectiveness, accomplishment, and belonging. It is an important factor in how we see ourselves; it colors our very sense of identity.

Work in organizations, directed toward achieving shared goals, also answers another human need: it allows us to feel useful. Individuals need to commit themselves to something that is valuable, that has a positive impact. Though usefulness is a highly subjective experience, it is linked to the particular objectives and causes that drive individuals to transcend their customary abilities. Because a search for usefulness—for meaning—largely determines a person's life course, it also influences life in organizations. Once again, this poses a challenge for the global leader: how to find a purpose or objective that employees from different cultures see as meaningful, inspiring them to strive in ways that simplistic formulas for return on investment and profit maximization cannot.

The dilemma facing organizations today is a serious one: breaking the old psychological contract means that in many organizations work is no longer an effective outlet for self-affirmation, identity formation, meaningful experience, and containment of anxiety. This dissolution of the traditional psychological contract raises a host of questions for organizational leaders: How can the motivational needs driving humankind's search for meaning and identity be integrated into modern organizational life? What can organizational leaders do to make people's existence in the company less stressful and more meaningful? In an age of organizational upheaval, how can the negative side effects of discontinuity be minimized? What can be done to give executives the kind of purpose that pushes them to stretch themselves? Although these questions challenge those at the helm of *any* organization, it is particularly difficult for global leaders to answer them, since these leaders must integrate and motivate people with diverse worldviews. The old psychological contract needs to be replaced; there is no doubt about that. But what is the new contract? Given the hurdles that have to be overcome, who are the new role models? What kinds of people possess the qualities to lead the global corporation of the future?

A ROAD MAP

As our earlier discussion reveals, we feel that CEOs currently face two critical issues: going global, and fostering employee loyalty at a time when organizations can no longer make meaningful long-term promises to their people. These issues probably sound very familiar to many readers of this book, from academicians and human resource professionals to executives of global organizations. In seeking solutions to these issues, we struggle with the question of how the corporation of the future will look. We ask ourselves what kind of leaders and what kind of organizations are role models in the global economy. Although we do not possess a crystal ball to tell us exactly what the future will bring, we believe that the CEOs profiled in this book provide partial answers to questions regarding effective leadership in the global economy.

We have built this book around three case studies that are already integrated into MBA courses and executive seminars around the world. Looking at the personal development of these three world-class leaders and the evolution of their organizations, we see how individuals are affected by corporate policy and get a glimpse of what it takes to be the leader of a global company. With that grounding, we then draw a description of a new organizational paradigm: what organizations will look like once the dust from reorganization and transformation settles.

Specifically, we look at how these three very successful business leaders brought their organizations through deep and discontinuous change processes to create truly global organizations. As a secondary theme, we look at what excellent leadership—whether global or domestic in scope—is all about. Toward that end, we examine the background and leadership style of each man, a process that reveals not only how global leadership skills develop but also how essential leadership is to organizations, and how central character is to leadership. Finally, in the conclusion, we first discuss the values that provide a foundation for excellence and a new psychological contract in vanguard companies such as Virgin, ABB, and BP and then show how these values can be translated into practice in any organization.

Introduction:
Global Leadership

Richard Branson and Virgin

Virgin is now one of the top five brand names in the United Kingdom. Its chairman and founder, Richard Branson, has become an international celebrity, the subject of numerous profiles in gossip magazines, in the business press, and on television. In the UK he has achieved folk-hero status and is frequently cited as a role model for young people wanting a successful business career. By the time he turned forty he was one of Britain's richest people, running an empire that encompasses travel (Virgin Atlantic), communications (books, radio and television stations, computer and video games), the retail business (Virgin Megastore), and hotels.

Percy Barnevik and ABB

In 1987, Percy Barnevik surprised the business community by announcing the creation of the world's largest cross-border merger: ASEA, a Swedish engineering group, and Brown Boveri, a Swiss company in the same field, were united to form ASEA Brown Boveri (ABB). With seventy companies in Europe and the United States, the merger created a $30 billion giant whose portfolio covered global markets for electric power generation and transmission equipment, high-speed trains, automation and robots, and environmental control systems. Since then, ABB has made an enormous impact on the business community, with its structure hailed as the organizational form of the future.

David Simon and British Petroleum

The situation facing David Simon when he took over British Petroleum (BP) in June 1992 was bleak. The organization desperately needed to revise its business strategy to reverse losses and repay billions of dollars in debt. Employees were demoralized following a derailed change attempt initiated by Simon's abrasive predecessor. Simon proved to be just the man to pick up and shake up the company, all the while maintaining his reputation and popularity as an affable, accessible leader. He implemented a straightforward plan to turn the organization around and achieved his financial goals a year ahead of schedule, which sent stockholder confidence soaring. Just as important, he restored employee confidence and boosted morale. He pulled his company together in a calming way, transforming the hard side of BP as well as the corporate culture.

At first glance, there are few obvious similarities among these three organizations, and even fewer among the CEOs. Branson is a *builder*, having created an organization from scratch. Barnevik, on the other hand, has been lauded for assembling the ultimate global organization: he is a highly effective *integrator*. Simon, whose prescription of bitter pills went a long way toward solving BP's health problems, is a *transformer*. Despite basic differences, however, these men display important similarities in their views of organizational design and of the role each plays in his company. They are first and foremost excellent leaders. But what exactly *is* an excellent leader, and why does excellent leadership make a difference?

LEADERS WHO MAKE A DIFFERENCE

In general, the most successful leaders simultaneously play two roles, one charismatic, the other more architectural. The first involves how leaders envision, empower, and energize to inspire and motivate their followers. The second involves strategies to improve organizational design and to control and reward employee behavior appropriately.

The charismatic, empowering role is the essence of leadership. The primary obligation of the leader is to determine where a company needs to go and then build commitment among followers to go in that direction. There can be no leadership without vision, without a vivid and well-communicated description of how the leader sees the organization in the future. All those who come within the leader's sphere of influence must align behind this vision, which is an expression of the organization's fundamental reason for being in the marketplace, its core values and beliefs, its mission (including qualitative and quantitative targets), and its strategic plans for accomplishing the mission.

To formulate a workable vision, leaders need the knack of perceiving salient trends in the environment. They must be able to process information from many different sources and use their perceptions as a basis for judging the direction in which environmental forces are propelling the organization. A close study of effective leaders reveals that they are much better than other people at managing cognitive complexity. This talent manifests itself in their gift for simplification, talent to digest large amounts of data, and ability to help others easily grasp highly complex issues.

If people are to be motivated, the leader's articulation of vision and mission has to be inspirational. Merely talking about increasing shareholders' wealth, or stressing the company's style ("We want to be fast followers"), is not enough. It is much more effective to find a niche in the market where one can be the best and then say so. The mission statement should be simple, yet it should stretch the minds and aspirations of all the company's executives.

The term *empowerment* is often used in this context of communicating both vision and expectations. Good leaders make empowerment of followers seem deceptively simple. There is, however, a trick: leaders who effectively empower followers not only express high performance expectations but also trust employees enough to give them the proper information (minimizing secrecy) to do an effective job. If employees believe that the leader has confidence in their ability to reach certain predetermined goals, and if they are given the responsibility and authority needed to attain those goals—in other words, if they are truly empowered—then employees do their utmost to oblige. By empowering followers, a leader enhances their self-esteem and feelings of self-confidence, often motivating them to perform well beyond expectations.

Unfortunately, empowerment of others is one of the areas in which leaders may be influenced negatively by their own character quirks. Those who are addicted to a sense of personal power, for example, are unable to give real power to others for fear of diminishing their own. Such leaders lack the generosity of vision to realize that by empowering followers they strengthen their organization and ultimately their own hold on power. This question of power—retaining it versus sharing it—is one of the issues that distinguish great leadership from dysfunctional leadership. Simon of BP has avoided the hubris of power. He projects himself as a friendly, even slightly self-effacing man. Until his surprise move into politics (he was named by Prime Minister Anthony Blair as minister for European trade and competitiveness in May 1997), he spent his entire career in BP, quietly working his way up the ranks, just part of the team. Because he has a teddy bear quality, he serves as a reassuring emotional "container" for his people, inspiring trust and effective communication. His colleagues describe him as a leader who encourages people to fill the spaces he leaves around him.

In every organization there is an enormous amount of free-floating, aggressive, and affectionate energy. Effective leaders know how to channel this energy in the right direction. It is important for aggressive energy to be directed externally; employees should not attack each other but fight the competition. Too much internally directed aggression manifests itself in an excess of political game playing within the organization. It helps to have an "enemy" to focus on while carrying out the organization's mission. Such a focus concentrates employee energies and helps to shape organizational identity. For this reason, successful companies watch their competitors very closely. While he was CEO of ABB, Barnevik constantly reminded his people of such enemies as Siemens, General Electric, Alcatel-Alstrom, Mitsubishi, and others, as in this example:

> It is not easy to explain to Swiss turbine workers why we are moving a certain technology to Poland. Especially not when we are in a recession and are having to cut down on employees in Western Europe. . . . [B]y establishing outposts there, we are opening up new markets in the East for ABB that may also result in increased sales from Switzerland. Then I say that we are actually competing with Mitsubishi. Poland and Switzerland together will be so strong that we can grab orders in Asia. Together we will be more competitive in the USA. And in Switzerland we can devote our skills to the more sophisticated components . . . while the less complicated parts are made in Poland. And in this way we can continue to pay high wages and salaries in Switzerland provided that productivity goes up sufficiently.[1]

Truly great leaders recognize that leadership is an art whose aim is to create an environment that stimulates and exhilarates, fostering excitement that leads employees to become completely absorbed in their tasks and achieve peak performance. Run by a flamboyant, intuitive, disarmingly friendly entrepreneur, Virgin has a corporate culture that puts high value on creativity and innovation. Branson has dressed up as Spiderman and Robin Hood—and even in drag—to promote his company, and he receives regular media attention as he tries to beat various speedboat and ballooning records. Like Peter Pan, he has a childlike *joie de vivre,* and he has made this trait part of Virgin's corporate culture. It is reflected even in the design of the organization: people at Virgin have a sense of control, a feeling of ownership in what they are doing, and they have the freedom to be playful in all that they do.

As this example shows, the envisioning, empowering, and energizing facets of the charismatic role need to be consolidated by the leader's architectural skills. While the charismatic qualities address people's inner theater—the *why* of work—the architectural concerns (organizational design, and control and reward systems) deal with the external world—the *way* people work. Barnevik is particularly strong in the role of organizational architect, as he showed in creating ABB. He is a soft-spoken, intense, philosophical Swede, a business school graduate and a specialist in data processing and information systems. He was one of the first to link many small companies from diverse national backgrounds into a network-based organization; it has proved to be much greater than the sum of its parts.

These three leaders exemplify the powerful and interactive combination of the charismatic and architectural roles within leadership: the charismatic component of leadership, which must also be concrete and focused; and the architectural component, which must have an element of flexibility and sensitivity.

LEADERS AS AGENTS OF CHANGE

The *quality* of leadership—the leader's ability to fulfill the roles described above—is particularly relevant in situations of strategic transformation and change. Leaders must not only prepare the organization (and the individuals in it) for change, and then carry the change through, but they must also maintain innovation and excitement in the organization after the process is completed. They must be visionaries who can build a solid construction on their foundational vision.

Charismatic leaders are by definition agents of change. What are the special characteristics that earn them the label *charismatic* and equip them with the ability to successfully bring about change? A wealth of literature answers this question. To summarize the discoveries:

- They display dissatisfaction with the status quo
- They are restless and energetic
- They are action-oriented
- Their discontent pushes them into searching for new opportunities
- They are entrepreneurial, impatient, and gifted at articulating a strategic vision, making the big picture seem within reach of their followers
- They are gifted at building alliances and making people feel special.

Leaders who fit this description stand out like beacons in the business world (as do those in the worlds of politics, art, and sport) as much for their rarity as for their brilliance.

The dilemma of leadership is that leaders of large organizations (unlike most of us mere mortals) must juggle both external forces and the powerful undertow of their own character and their employees'. Of course, environmental forces do play an important role in organizational life—each industry has its particular characteristics—but organizations are microcosms of human social life, and underestimating the personal factor produces unbalanced analysis. The style and character of a CEO has a considerable impact on his or her company, for better or worse. Far from being simple reagents in a predictable formula, excellent leaders have the capacity to transform strategic constraints into new challenges, influencing organizational culture and providing direction in their vital role as catalyst of change.

Such leaders know that for the change process to move forward, every individual must be fully engaged and truly empowered, believing himself or herself to be crucial. Employees who are inspired, empowered, and free to act stretch themselves to make exceptional efforts, have a high degree of commitment, and are willing to take risks. This type of employee performance simultaneously drives the change process and reinforces the new basis of the organization. The blueprint of the change process is identification with the leader's abilities and ideals, and a shared vision; the bricks and mortar are communication, trust, and reward. If the leader does not allow open communication, there is no trust, and the change process founders.

The three leaders profiled here instill in their organizations the premise that change is a given. They lay the groundwork for continuous change, so no one is caught unaware or unprepared. Cultivating a positive attitude toward change is critical because of the danger of complacency in the face of external danger signs, and the risk of resistance. As the saying goes, "Nothing kills like success." Employees come to realize that change is a permanent aspect of their organization, not a temporary state. As a result, they are less likely to resist change.

Indeed, the first two major challenges for a company in the process of change are motivating people to function effectively in an unpredictable environment and managing the opposing dynamic of resistance. As Barnevik pointed out: "It is rather traumatic to make this sort of move [the merger of ASEA and BBC]. It takes a lot of determination, a lot of perseverance, because it is always easier to be against something than to be for something. We are conservative animals, we like the past, we like the historical."[2]

LEARNING FROM THREE EXCELLENT LEADERS

Throughout the rest of this book, we look closely at the three leaders introduced here. Each leader's story is used to illustrate the charismatic and architectural aspects of leadership. The Virgin case study is of a company built on a culture of continuous change. The unflagging creativity, innovation, and entrepreneurship that Richard Branson champions in his organization—those characteristics that define Virgin's corporate culture—are an important key to Virgin's success. We also take a close look at Branson the man, discussing how his character has molded Virgin's corporate culture. The ABB case—the story of a record-breaking merger and the process of integration that followed—shows how Percy Barnevik's personal history affected his organization. The last case study addresses David Simon's time at British Petroleum, where he engineered one of the most successful corporate transformations of the nineties—remaining throughout the process a calm, likable man trusted by employees and shareholders alike. The case also presents a before-and-after picture, describing at some length the situation at BP before Simon became CEO and then looking at how John Browne, his successor (a man who has affirmed his commitment to flexibility and learning in an organization that was once about as limber and modern as a dinosaur) built upon Simon's legacy.

This is not meant to be a linear book. It is organized so that the introductory chapter to each case analyzes a critical aspect of the organization; but quite often the points that are raised in one case are relevant to the others, as well as being more generally pertinent. We hope you will keep in mind the insights gained from one case as you study the others. We would like you to become aware of the extent to which leaders' dreams and aspirations affect the architecture of their organizations. We want you to recognize how powerfully a leader's inner theater (as influenced by his or her early childhood experiences) can influence organizational design.

As you read, ask yourself some questions. How are Branson's and Simon's developmental experiences reflected in their leadership style? How does Barnevik encourage creativity in his highly technical organization? Is the definition of creativity different within an engineering or petrochemical firm from that of the highly diverse empire that is Virgin? How has Branson kept all the creativity and entrepreneurship in his organization from turning into chaos? What are the similarities between Barnevik's and Branson's organizations?

What about corporate transformation? All three men, in varying degrees and varying ways, have transformed their organizations. After reading the case study about Simon and BP—the one most explicitly about change—reflect on the previous two and how Barnevik and Branson also introduced change, though less explicitly. Judge for yourself what works, and in what situation. For example, what did Barnevik do to make integration of ASEA and Brown Boveri so seamless a process?

You might want to read through the case studies more than once, looking at each one from various perspectives. In reading the interviews, try to tease out clues to the men's personalities and leadership styles, for example. Would you like to work with one of these men? What is unique about each person's style? Whose style do you prefer, and why? As you will discover, the three case studies and interviews are rich in detail. Looking closely at them from different points of view should prove revealing.

Of course, we cannot all become charismatic leaders and architects of global organizations. But we can draw on our observation of exceptional leaders—on the skills we see them employ and the actions we see them take—and learn from them how to improve our own leadership abilities, identify challenges, and formulate a strategic vision and align others behind it. We can watch how they create corporate cultures that embody the new psychological contract, and try to replicate the process in our own firms. It is in the interest of organizational survival—which requires exceptional performance, commitment, and innovation from everybody involved—that we do so.

The New
Global Leaders

⊕ PART ONE

Richard Branson

CHAPTER ONE

Richard Branson
The Builder

Richard Branson began his career as a teenage business prodigy in the late 1960s. Over the past thirty years, various adjectives have been appended to his name, all more or less derogatory: "precocious," "hippie," "fun-loving," "lucky." As his entertainment empire grew and diversified, and his competitors were forced to take him seriously, deprecating epithets began to lose their force. However, one has stuck: "youthful," despite the fact that in the year 2000 Branson will celebrate his fiftieth birthday.

From a schoolboy venture into publishing, he has built an international entertainment and leisure empire and is now one of the most successful and wealthiest individuals in the world. His organization is maturing, and so is he. Although nobody is old at fifty in the western world, it is a time of life when most people plan retirement, slow down, anticipate grandchildren, and begin to feel the weight of accumulated responsibilities. Richard Branson, however, is still up to his old tricks. What sort of organization and personal image will he carry into the first decade of the new century? Has Peter Pan begun to grow up? Is he developing from the *enfant terrible* of British business into an organizational *paterfamilias*?

As we shall see with Percy Barnevik, it is clear that family background provides a key to Branson's success. The notion of "family" is critical to how he has built up and characterizes his organization. When he says "People are our greatest asset," he is not just paying lip service to the general public. His business maxim is staff first, customers second, and shareholders third. Branson believes that his employees should be given top priority. He has created a friendly, egalitarian, nonhierarchical, familylike atmosphere in all of his companies, an ambiance in which people have fun and enjoy themselves. Once a year he gives a big party at his family home in Oxfordshire to which every Virgin employee is invited. He is also unapologetic about his willingness to employ members of his family in top positions, shrugging off accusations of nepotism. Though the case study that follows examines Branson's early life in some detail, it is worth emphasizing this point here. In a healthy family, an individual blossoms and begins to define himself or herself within a secure and affectionate psychological and physical space. In many ways, the family is the first organizational model a person encounters. Virgin's culture—a creative and entrepreneurial preserve—replicates those values with which Branson grew up and that helped form his personality.

When he nominates his people as Virgin's greatest asset, Branson points adroitly to something that gives a corporation a long-term, inimitable competitive edge: the creative talent of its individual employees. Competitors can catch up on core competencies. Benchmarking and reengineering may put them on the cutting edge. But only individuals can continuously produce new, important, and exciting ideas that allow a company to reinvent itself, enable it to manage for self-renewal, and create a true learning organization.

Although possibly the most valuable asset for any corporation, creative talent is probably also the most unrealized. Creative people are thought to be nonconformist, unpredictable, self-absorbed, and therefore difficult to manage. Because many organizations are filled with conformists, and conformists tend to like other conformists, the frustrations and limitations of such organizations drive creative people out—to the organization's loss. Attracting, developing, and keeping maverick talents is a major challenge to any leader. It is essential to create an environment that offers a high degree of freedom and encourages original ideas.

Branson has risen to this challenge by building his businesses through organic growth rather than acquisition. Growing and starting new companies enables him to stretch his people, and he enjoys providing opportunity for his employees. At the risk of overplaying the image, this strategy fits his concept of the organizational family, one that grows by progeny rather than by adoption.

As with many entrepreneurial organizations, it is impossible to separate Branson's personal image from that of Virgin. His style, face, and personality (the "grinning pullover," to his detractors) are inextricably linked to his company. This is something he has deliberately contrived. Branson's sense of fun has lulled competitors into thinking that he is not a serious businessman. Lord King, then chairman of British Airways, admitted after his airline received a bruising from Branson in 1987 that if the latter had worn a pair of steel-rimmed glasses and a double-breasted suit and shaved off his beard, he (Lord King) would have taken him more seriously. Branson did later shave off his beard and put in contact lenses—and dress in drag to launch a new collection of Virgin bridal wear. This sort of stunt may make the business establishment writhe, but nowadays they are forced to shake off their irritation and look immediately to their bottom line. Such showmanship and image building, though, has its flip side. Entrepreneurs rarely pass on their heritage successfully, and this extraordinarily intense identification of the company with its chairman worries observers, in the same way that observers wondered about the future of ABB after Barnevik. Without Branson, can Virgin maintain the position it now enjoys?

Speculation about Virgin without Branson has to be serious, given his penchant for risking his neck in daredevil adventures: breaking the record for crossing the Atlantic in a speedboat, attempting to go around the world by hot air balloon (both stunts very nearly cost him his life), and abseiling down high-rise buildings. The personal challenges Branson sets himself are increasingly seen as a liability for Virgin, despite the extremely high profile they lend to the company. People seem to have trouble deciding what to think of him. In 1997, a national opinion poll revealed Branson to be the nation's favorite candidate for president, should Britain ever become a republic—a result one journalist appears to have taken seriously enough to use as the basis for his article:

> Many of [Branson's] contemporaries in today's world of business spend much of their time reducing risks. Mr. Branson, by contrast, pursues a course designed to increase risks, particularly to his own neck. In the age of "safety first," this, coupled with a gift—some might call it an over-indulged taste—for self-promotion and a flamboyant style, gives him a certain panache. He strikes many as a

heroic figure, otherwise scarce in today's public life. Indeed, in quarters guided largely by erratic opinion polls about our constitutional prospects, Mr. Branson is held to be a suitable president if ever Britain becomes a republic. It is a curious fact that people who would not dream of going up in a hot air balloon, even for a short outing, see great virtue in a man who wants to go round the world in one. In the confidence that a monarchy will continue to serve this country's best interests for the foreseeable future, we have not given much thought to the specifications required for a president. We, too, see merit in the sort of exploits Mr. Branson undertakes with hot air balloons, but we reserve doubt about whether such exploits mark him out as a man best suited to what has been referred to as "the endless adventure of governing men." The British admire boldness in the air. They prefer to be ruled by people who keep both feet on the ground.[1]

Richard Branson seems to be quite happy living with the apparent contradictions in his personal life (the family man who nevertheless regularly risks widowing his wife and orphaning his children) and in his company's portfolio. Recent new ventures include the launch of Virgin Cola, cosmetics (Vie), Virgin Bride, and clothing lines (consistent with Virgin's roots in the youth market). He returned to his origins in the music business when he launched a new record company in 1996, called, naturally, V2. Personal finance services are another new venture for Branson. They include pension plans, advertisements for which feature Branson himself that read: "As you get older you get wiser. (Get a pension now while you're still relatively stupid.)" The Virgin voice still sounds clearly, although the volume appears to have been turned down. (Branson commented that his second venture into the music industry with V2 would be less hectic than his first with Virgin Records; at age forty-six, he couldn't see himself out clubbing until all hours the way he did twenty years ago.) However, continued diversification of Virgin's businesses raises questions about the company's ability to maintain the synergy between its various parts. So should his flamboyance be controlled? Is he the clown of the business world, or a trainee ringmaster?

In 1993, Branson gave a speech to the British Institute of Directors. His audience no doubt expected to be amused. Instead, the speech began: "Let me share with you the philosophy behind our experiences at Virgin. The basic principles are 'People matter' and 'Small is beautiful.' From there, I'd go on to say: shape the enterprise around the people; build businesses, don't buy them; be the best, not the biggest; capture every fleeting idea; drive for change; and, a very practical point, persuade the government of the merits of competition."

What followed was a serious and masterly statement of Virgin's business values and practices. Nobody hearing it could remain in doubt of Branson's determination as an intensely competitive and tough businessman. The rebellious schoolboy had come a long way.

Chapter Two, "Branson's Virgin," provides an opportunity to explore the person-organization interface. From a developmental point of view, it examines the making of an entrepreneur. Virgin represents effective leadership of continuous change in the context of an entrepreneurial organization and, finally, raises questions about the future of an organization that is strongly identified with its founder.

The case of Virgin focuses on leadership in a creative, entrepreneurial organization. Virgin has made many brilliant moves, from signing Mike Oldfield (of *Tubular Bells* fame) to taking on the world with Virgin Atlantic Airways. The group has also weathered spectacular setbacks, beginning in the early days with Branson's brief imprisonment for tax fraud; more recently, the company went public and then private again within two years. The case offers insight into these and other management issues that have come to the fore in Virgin's history. Among them are transition from entrepreneurial to more professional management; formulation of strategy for, and management of, rapid growth, particularly expansion into unrelated areas and overseas; management of strategic alliances; development of a corporate culture centered around youth, informality, and adventure; preference for promotion of insiders who fit rather than outside candidates; and management of creativity.

What sets Virgin apart from other successful and visible organizations is Richard Branson himself. He has had no formal business training; his leadership style is more or less an extension of his personality. A case study of Virgin would be incomplete, therefore, without an examination of the man at the heart of the organization. What made him the person he is? What developmental experiences were important to him? How does his personality affect his organization? How did he become an entrepreneur? How has he managed to avoid the pitfalls of entrepreneurship: narcissism and hubris?

All the evidence suggests that Branson does not have hanging around his neck the albatross that usually accompanies entrepreneurship: he does not seem to be overly preoccupied with control and appears to be capable of delegation. However, he is certainly no stranger to narcissistic needs, as the publicity focused on his person indicates. But his narcissism seems to be within reasonable, functional boundaries. His wife, old friends, and selected family members play an important role in maintaining his psychological balance.

Branson is regularly cited as a role model by young people who hope to be successful in business careers without having to compromise their personal ethics. His charisma derives mainly from personal warmth and obvious liking for people, which is felt by most who meet him. He possesses a unique combination of energy, originality, shrewdness, and, last but not least, luck.

It is often through sheer perseverance that Branson has prevailed against the odds. If something feels right to him, he concludes that it is probably worth doing and commits himself to it until the project is accomplished. This does not mean that he rushes headlong into ventures without first analyzing the risk. On the contrary, he has developed his own framework—intuitive as it may be—for evaluating new ventures and their attendant uncertainties. This quality gives a Janus face to his behavior. He is a warm, relaxed, friendly family man, but at the same time an extremely competitive workaholic who can be a very tough but brilliant negotiator.

His personal philosophy is, "Life is short; one has to make the most of it. Thus, do things that you like. If your work and your hobby are the same, you will work long hours because you are motivated." Much of this philosophy is reflected in how he sees his role as an organizational architect. His philosophy of management has proved to be highly effective; his sprawling business empire is an impressive achievement. In spite of all the hype, Branson's leadership style and the manner in which he manages the Virgin Group warrant serious attention. His story is a fascinating tale of high-performance leadership that provides unique insight into the nature of the person-organization interface.

The case also examines the basic issue of the future of the Virgin Group, with or without Richard Branson. Although he denies it, at times he seems to have some kind of death wish. Will his leadership style eventually become dysfunctional? Most important, what would happen to the Virgin Group if its charismatic chairman were no longer associated with the company?

As you read the case, think about whether you would like to work at Virgin. What elements of the company do you find attractive? Which might put you off? What problems do you see? Consider the lengths to which Branson goes to foster creativity in his organization, encourage rapid action, and be personally available to his employees. You might want later to compare his attitude to that of Percy Barnevik—both cases touch on similar issues. We suggest that you reconsider these questions once you have read the Branson interview; do any of your answers and opinions change?

CHAPTER TWO

Branson's Virgin

"THE VOICE OF YOUTH"[1]

In the summer of 1967, the headmaster of Stowe, an exclusive English boys' private school with a liberal reputation, faced a familiar dilemma. A seventeen-year-old student wished to leave before taking his final exams so that he could pursue nonacademic interests. The boy, Richard, wished to develop his growing magazine business, which he was operating in his spare time using fellow students as workers and a nearby public pay phone as his office. Sensing the young man's determination, and having discussed the matter with his parents, the headmaster finally agreed to the boy's leaving. At the time he was not sanguine about the boy's prospects and told him he would either end up in prison or a millionaire. Both prophecies were to prove correct. Looking back today, the headmaster can claim to have played a small part in launching one of Britain's fastest-growing private companies—led by his ex-student, the unconventional and flamboyant Richard Branson.

Branson's brainchild, *Student* magazine, was a product of the 1960s, the decade when the postwar baby boomers came of age. Across Western Europe and North America, young people enjoyed educational, employment, and lifestyle opportunities unknown to their parents, all made possible by rapid economic growth. The decade became known for its promotion of youth culture, in which authority was challenged, fashions changed rapidly, and rock stars were the global gurus of a new age.

It was in such a climate that young Richard, tired of the boring inadequacies of the traditional school magazine and recognizing a potential market, founded his own publication. Aimed at readers aged sixteen to twenty-five, *Student* was to be the "Voice of Youth." Its eclectic style reflected the founder's ability to commission articles by celebrities and to identify subjects not touched by many well-established magazines. Norman Mailer, Vanessa Redgrave, and Jean-Paul Sartre, for example, all contributed pieces that appeared among articles on sex and rock music, interviews with terrorists, and proposals for educational reform.

The initial success of the magazine (Branson optimistically claimed it had a circulation of one hundred thousand) prompted favorable notice in the national press. Branson was described in complimentary terms as being a kind of one-man band: editor, publisher, and sole advertising manager. He had a reputation for being a professional whose enthusiasm got things done, to an extent that put older and more experience competitors to shame. Certainly his energy and enthusiasm were needed to keep the organization going. The offices were transient, first located in a friend's basement flat, later in a disused church. The staff—who in effect were a loosely organized cooperative of friends, acquaintances, and hangers-on who turned up to help—distributed magazines, took copy, and, frequently, screened out creditors. The staff were not paid a salary; Branson just supplied them with a place to sleep and some food. They were not working so much for him as with him.

Not yet twenty years old, Branson found himself with the responsibilities of a much older person, employing ten people directly, walking a fine line between solvency and financial disaster, interviewing celebrities and appearing on television, and rarely relaxing except to chase girls and indulge in escapades with his immediate circle.

Despite his hedonistic lifestyle, and the casual organization of the magazine, Branson always focused on business. His drive and facility for promotion were not enough, however, and *Student* magazine was not the financial success that Branson had expected. Seeking new activities to boost his flagging business, he decided to try to tap the potential in selling records, still overpriced even though the British government was no longer maintaining retail prices (to support certain industries by allowing manufacturers and suppliers to "recommend" prices to retailers).

Lacking the capital to start a retail outlet, Branson and his associates simply placed an advertisement in the last issue of *Student* to test the market, listing the records likely to appeal to young people. The product range was mostly that of bands and singers on the fringe of the music world whose recordings were often available only in London stores specializing in alternative music. Most important, prices undercut those offered in stores by as much as 15 percent. Orders—with cash—came flooding in. Using the cash to place volume orders with record companies prior to shipping to his customers, Branson found he had created a cut-price mail-order record supply business that required little initial investment or working capital and that enjoyed a significant competitive advantage over established retail chains.

Casting around for a name for his new business, Branson rejected ideas that evoked the music and recording business, since even at that time he was thinking toward a future in which he would create a global brand that would not be limited to entertainment. He finally accepted a joking suggestion from one of his coterie that what they needed was a name proclaiming their commercial innocence but also having a certain shock value, in keeping with the antiestablishment mood of the times. What better name, therefore, than "Virgin"?

It was not long before Virgin Records was attracting the attention of the major recording companies, suspicious of the upstart's large orders and pricing policy. Investigations led to an immediate ban on direct-credit sales, which Branson then successfully circumnavigated by using a small retail chain as a purchasing agent.

But other problems arose. He quickly realized that buying and selling records in bulk required proper controls and systems. He turned therefore to a childhood friend, Nik Powell, to help him manage his new business, offering in return a 40 percent stake in the company. Methodical where Branson was erratic, cautious where Branson would overextend himself, Powell became the ideal counterbalance in the record company, ensuring customers' orders were correct, payments made, and staff properly deployed. With a competitive advantage in a growing market and a semblance of administration on a low-cost base, the mail-order company seemed set for success. Ever eager to expand, Branson considered all the possibilities: recording studios, music publishing, retail shops, perhaps even record production and artist management. But his plans were upset by immediate problems brought about by hard luck and folly.

Branson's first setback came early in 1971, when a national postal strike threatened to push the company into bankruptcy. Immediately Branson rented retail space in Oxford Street, London's main shopping thoroughfare, transferred his stock of records there, and launched Virgin Retail. True to the emerging Virgin style, the shop's decor was a mix of the outrageous and the shabby, attracting customers more bent on enjoying an experience than on spending money. As the retail chain expanded into provincial towns and cities, Powell, on periodic visits, found that, left to themselves, Virgin's shops would become the meeting place of pot-smoking music freaks.

Having reacted successfully to his company's first major challenge, Branson was stopped in his tracks when he made a misguided business decision—one that led to temporary imprisonment. In the summer of 1971, Virgin received its first foreign order. A Belgian company ordered a van load of records, which, since they were intended for export, could be purchased by Virgin tax-free. Branson, wanting to learn more about overseas markets, decided to make the delivery personally. However, because of a misunderstanding over shipment papers, he found himself back in England with the records *and* with documents showing that they had been "exported." Tempted by quick cash profit, Branson sold the "exported" records through his London store. Four or five more bogus trips followed, until the tax authorities pounced. Shocked and humiliated, Branson spent an uncomfortable night in Dover prison, to be released only after a tearful appeal to his parents to put up the £30,000 bail. They had to use their home as security. Eventually, formal charges were dropped in return for an out-of-court financial settlement (a down payment of £15,000; and taxes, duties, and charges of £38,000 payable over the next three years), the usual procedure in such cases. Later, Branson would laughingly dismiss his night in a cell, but the pain and embarrassment he caused his parents made him resolve to avoid sleepless nights and pay taxes. Even so, he remains an unwilling taxpayer and keeps his Virgin shareholding in offshore family trusts, preferring to reinvest all the profits in the business.

While these setbacks were taking place, Branson had a stroke of luck that was perhaps not evident at the time. Simon Draper, a distant relation from South Africa, arrived at Virgin looking for a job in England to avoid military service back home. A university graduate with left-of-center views, Draper was passionately interested in, and knowledgeable about, popular music. He joined Virgin as a record buyer, learning the record business from the bottom up.

In later years, Draper earned himself the nickname "Mr. Golden Ears," the industry's accolade for a successful record producer in recognition of the ability to spot and develop bands and singers having potential. He earned his place at Virgin by persuading Branson to consider backing a nervous and troubled young musician who arrived at Virgin clutching a handful of recording tapes. Already rejected by the major recording studios, the young man was looking for friends and supporters. Mike Oldfield found both at Virgin, and his first recording, *Tubular Bells,* was to launch him and Virgin into the big time.

TUBULAR BELLS

Mike Oldfield was a talented and experienced musician with his own vision of popular music. Dismissive of stereotypical rock bands with a vocalist and backing musicians, Oldfield wanted to be known for music that met his artistic standards irrespective of its general appeal and commercial success. Not surprisingly, such an uncompromising attitude deterred potential backers.

Branson and Draper, however, were intrigued by the demonstration tapes Oldfield produced. They suggested to the musician that he live at the Manor while developing his work. This was a recording studio with the latest recording technology in a country house near Oxford that Virgin had recently purchased and converted. The result, after a year's endeavors, was *Tubular Bells,* an original recording of instrumental sound effects, one overlaying another, to create a blended harmonic theme. Released in 1973, it was an immediate and substantial best-seller, eventually selling more than five million copies worldwide. For Branson, this was the ideal opportunity to launch the Virgin Record label and join the ranks of the small independent record producers active in the UK market at that time.

Oldfield contracted with Virgin to produce his music, and with Branson to act as his manager. This was an unusual arrangement in the popular music industry, where artists and record labels are frequently in dispute. Indeed, Oldfield was later to sue Virgin for imposition of unfair contracts, a tactic often employed by rock bands in an attempt to renegotiate contract terms once success has been achieved. In Oldfield's case, the matter was settled out of court, and he remained with Virgin until 1992. He never repeated the huge success of his first title, although his music is still much in demand for film and television soundtracks.

With Oldfield, the Virgin Record label had its first success; the massive inflow of funds transformed the company. No longer constrained by lack of capital, Branson began to diversify and rationalize his company, starting businesses in fashion retailing and catering, while closing down the mail-order operation. Popular music, however, remained Virgin's *raison d'être*.

Under Simon Draper's creative direction, the record label began to expand, initially focusing on artists outside the mainstream wherever Draper's interests lay. Such a policy fit the Virgin image but restricted profit potential. Within two years, however, financial pressure forced Virgin to reassess its position to avoid becoming a one-hit record label. Branson, by now anxious to sign up any artist likely to give his company credibility, put all his wheeler-dealer skills into creating deals with the financial backing and distribution rights that would be attractive to the bands he needed.

Serious attempts were made to sign up such big names as David Bowie, Pink Floyd, and the Who, as well as lesser artists who seemed to have breached the barrier between obscurity and fame. Never one to be deterred by reputation (or any other obstacle that would deter most people), Branson even approached the Rolling Stones—and nearly got them. All these efforts, however, led nowhere, and Branson became increasingly concerned. He needed something fast to reestablish the Virgin name with the record-buying public. He achieved his aim with a notorious punk rock band: the Sex Pistols.

Debauched and drug-crazed, foul-mouthed and obscene, the Sex Pistols cultivated a reputation of anarchical outrage, both on and off the stage. The public in general, and parents in particular, were scandalized and the band was angrily denounced by pundits, politicians, and religious leaders. Their record *God Save the Queen,* which derided the British royal family, only added to the furor. Predictably, young people flocked to buy their records and attend their performances.

Draper had severe misgivings about associating the record label with a band of such notoriety and, in his view, dubious talent. But Branson was excited by the prospect, even though admitting privately that their music was dreadful. When the Sex Pistols were dropped in a panic by more conservative record labels, Virgin signed them up. For eighteen months in 1977–78, Virgin and the Sex Pistols were the subject of intense media coverage and speculation, until the band disintegrated when one of its members, already facing a murder charge, died of a drug overdose. Their short existence was a considerable fillip for Virgin, though. Over time, Virgin was to sign the biggest names in British and international rock, and in 1993 it finally netted the biggest of them all: the Rolling Stones.

The music business was in turn complemented by more recording studios and retail outlets, music and book publishing, nightclubs, and cinemas as the company expanded. In the United States, by far the largest market for popular music, a Virgin subsidiary was formed in 1978 to promote Virgin's UK artists and attract new talent. Previously, many artists had been reluctant to sign with Virgin because they felt that without a significant U.S. presence the company did not have the strength to successfully represent them worldwide.

All in all, Branson could look back with some satisfaction as he prepared his company for the 1980s. Virgin had grown profitably, and his expansion plans all seemed to fit comfortably around the core of the business, popular music. But the music business was heading for a slump that would again test Branson's entrepreneurial skill. This time, however, his solutions included action that seemed the complete antithesis to the Virgin ethos: people would have to be fired.

VIRGIN IN THE 1980s

The record industry had shown average annual growth rates of 20 percent throughout most of the 1970s. But as the decade closed, recession and high inflation, combined with changing consumer tastes, severely affected the music business worldwide. Sales contracted, and few record companies earned profits. Virgin registered losses of £400,000 in 1980, and £900,000 in 1981. Although well established, the record company was still a small player in a business dominated by large multinationals. Moreover, it was still largely dependent on the UK market, lacking a broad geographical base that could have stabilized revenue.

Virgin was similarly positioned in the retail business. With sixteen outlets, Virgin was the third largest specialist retailer in the UK, competing against other specialists as well as multiple stores.

With financial pressure mounting, Branson was forced to act. He looked to Nik Powell to find solutions that, inevitably, were likely to prove difficult. Working in conjunction with consultants, Powell recommended a series of cost-cutting measures, including dismissing some staff—a task that Branson has always found daunting and avoids, usually by delegating, if possible. Virgin personnel had grown accustomed to a degree of job security in return for modest salaries and their flexible approach to working, neither of which were common in the music industry. Moreover, in keeping with the familial feeling Branson tried to encourage, people expected to be moved around until they found their niche rather than be dismissed. People were not fired—at least they had not been until now. But on this occasion the unthinkable happened, and the anxiety and ill-feeling that it caused led to talk of union representation. Virgin staff felt that Branson had become too isolated and knew little of their routine concerns. A shocked Branson immediately instigated staff meetings and a salary review, particularly for those with lower incomes. His response proved sufficient to dampen dissent.

To some extent, Branson himself inflamed the discontent in his company. His personal business philosophy was simple: why worry about the past; it is over and done; look to the future to solve difficulties through new opportunities, expansion, and growth. On the one hand the company was firing staff, closing its U.S. office, cutting its roster of bands and singers, and writing off unprofitable capital investments; but on the other, Branson was using scarce financial resources to purchase two nightclubs, Heaven (London's largest venue for homosexuals) and the struggling Roof Garden. He also launched a new London entertainment guide, *Event,* founded in response to a troubled rival magazine, *Time Out.* In the summer of 1981, *Time Out* was off the streets for some time as a result of a strike. Branson saw an opportunity to challenge a monopoly supplier and return to publishing, a business activity for which he had particular enthusiasm. However, ill-prepared and requiring more cash than expected, *Event* quickly became a liability to Virgin when a revitalized *Time Out* and another new rival magazine entered the market. Within a year, *Event* closed, at a cost to Virgin of £750,000.

Branson's actions also created tension among his senior management. Draper and other long-serving executives saw some of his moves as folly. Powell especially was angered by what he saw as profligacy in tight times; he felt that Branson's actions could put the whole Virgin enterprise in jeopardy. His working relationship with Branson soured; he realized that his ambitions were likely to be unfulfilled while he was number two. Matters came to a head over creative policy.

Despite limited funds, Draper wanted to invest in new bands and to carry on financing existing artists whom he believed would eventually be profitable. Powell followed a more cautious, corporatist approach and pressed for pruning of money-losing bands. Seeing the necessity to make a choice and settle matters, Branson, with some reluctance and sadness, backed Draper's artistic judgment rather than the traditional approach offered by Powell.

His instinct proved right since, within a short space of time, Virgin signed up some of the most profitable bands of the eighties: Phil Collins, Human League, Simple Minds, and in particular the hugely successful Culture Club, led by the controversial Boy George.

Virgin had successfully maneuvered itself out of the recession, nearly doubling its turnover from £48 million in 1982 to £94 million in 1983, with profits soaring to over £11 million. But Nik Powell was not around to share the success. Dissatisfied with his position, he had left the company in 1981, selling his stock in return for a package comprising a £1 million payment, Virgin's cinema interests, and a video recording studio (which later became the core of Palace Pictures, the UK's largest independent film production company in the 1980s).

Branson was once again the 100 percent owner of Virgin, with two trusted lieutenants, Simon Draper and Ken Berry, a long-standing collaborator. Branson depended on Draper for creative decisions and on Berry for contracts and management. Branson's own role was to talk to Draper and Berry several times a day, and to appear in person to sign stars to the record label. (Draper and Berry later acquired holdings in the company after lengthy negotiations.) Virgin was massively profitable and rapidly expanding. In France, Germany, and Italy, Virgin distribution companies were established to add local artists to the company roster and to represent UK bands. In the United States, the Virgin label was reestablished. Moreover, the huge success of Virgin artists attracted increasing numbers of established and emerging bands to the Virgin stable, creating a momentum that challenged the industry leaders.

In circumstances such as these, traditional business practice would dictate that success be consolidated and expansion restricted to complementary activities. Such, however, was not to be Branson's way. He wanted to expand his company in a completely new direction. To the astonishment of music industry observers, the horror of Simon Draper, and the ridicule of the music press, Richard Branson was off on a new path. He was going to found an airline.

"THE AIRLINE THAT BOY GEORGE BUILT"

In early 1984, Branson received a call from Randolph Fields, a thirty-one-year-old Californian-born lawyer who had founded British Atlantic, a cut-rate, transatlantic airline that existed only on paper. Fields was seeking additional financing to get his carrier airborne. Branson was all too aware of the dangers in entering the airline business: his company had no experience, it was capital-intensive, and revenue was highly seasonal. Perhaps most of all, he recalled the recent experience of another such UK venture, Laker Airlines, that had been pushed into bankruptcy by high debts, currency fluctuations, and ferocious competition from established national airlines. The industry's Goliaths had slaughtered the upstart David, the echoes of which still caused strain in UK and U.S. trade diplomacy.

Yet, despite all these reservations and obstacles, Branson was persuaded by Field's proposal. Within a week ("We can decide something in the morning and have it running in the afternoon" is Branson's proud boast) they formed a partnership, renaming the airline Virgin Atlantic—later to be dubbed "the airline that Boy George built," a reference to the supposed source of cash injected by Branson into his new project.

In March 1984, the airline had neither a license to fly nor any aircraft; it had a staff of one and no offices. Under the circumstances, Branson's target of a June inaugural flight to catch the summer season seemed to be unachievable. But after battles with regulatory authorities over a license, and protracted negotiations with Boeing to purchase an ex-Aerolíneas Argentinas 747 on a sale-or-return contract backed by a complex leasing agreement with a U.S. bank, the airline gained some credibility.

Virgin Atlantic's low fares began to attract customers. They were served by a staff that soon numbered nearly one hundred, all rapidly recruited and trained, including several ex-Laker managers who brought with them their experience in running a low-cost operation. Branson's aim of launching an airline in three months seemed to be coming true. Pushing himself close to a breakdown, Branson drove the whole enterprise forward, involving himself in every detail of the airline. He was rewarded by a successful launch on June 22, 1984, at which he played to the cameras dressed as a World War I pilot in leather jacket and goggles. Virgin Atlantic was off the ground.

Creating his airline took Branson into unfamiliar territory. His business demanded new skills not required in the unregulated, open-market environment of the record industry. By contrast, the airline business is highly political: being awarded jealously guarded international landing rights to (mostly) nationalized airlines involves protracted intergovernmental negotiations. To launch his airline, Branson was forced to lobby British ministers to obtain their support and protection in his dealings with U.S. government agencies and UK regulatory authorities.

Branson also had an eye to the future, expecting predatory pricing from the likes of British Airways and Pan Am that would jeopardize his cost advantage, particularly in the winter months. Such pricing, he knew, needed both U.S. and UK government approval and could only be stopped by politicians. On his own, he would be powerless in a price war with the large transatlantic carriers, who could subsidize one loss-making route from their other ticket revenues. That would be the Laker scenario all over again.

As predicted, the winter of 1984 saw a transatlantic fare war between British Airways and Virgin Atlantic in the UK, and Pan Am and People Express (an operation similar to Virgin Atlantic that in some ways was the model for Branson's airline) in the United States. British ministers in the right-of-center Thatcher government were in a dilemma. On the one hand, they supported an open-skies competition policy that benefited the consumer through lower fares, but on the other they saw equally the need to protect new entrants to the market, without which there could be only limited competition. Branson used his newly found diplomatic skills to exploit this dilemma; his lobbying, plus the threat of an antitrust suit in the United States, created sufficient uncertainty and confusion to force the UK transport minister to rescind cut-rate fares already agreed upon with British Airways. It was a short-term victory, but at least it forced the large carriers to be circumspect in their opposition to Branson.

Thanks to the blunted competition, Virgin Atlantic attracted enough passengers in the difficult winter months to keep flying and to end its first financial year marginally in profit. Randolph Fields, the originator of the airline idea, did not stay with Virgin very long, however. His leadership style did not fit either the Virgin ethos or the detailed operation of an airline, although Branson recognized Fields's contribution in putting together the initial proposal. Press reports of a board room bust-up were publicly discounted by Branson. But behind the scenes, relations became increasingly acrimonious, until Branson felt forced to act and ousted Fields from the board in late 1984. In 1985, he bought out Field's share of the business for £1 million. Fields later said that he had fallen in love with Branson on the day they met, but that Branson had only fallen in love with his (Fields's) idea.

"FROM THE ROCK MARKET TO THE STOCK MARKET"

In late 1986, a series of press and TV advertisements appeared in the UK under the title "From the Rock Market to the Stock Market." The ads invited the public to buy stock in the Virgin Group. Richard Branson—for so long a champion of private company status and the independence of entrepreneurs—had succumbed to the blandishments of City investment bankers to sell part of his company. Such deal making was an intrinsic part of the investment-banking process, and in the mid-1980s, as the UK market was experiencing a powerful bull market, it was easy to understand the temptation for successful entrepreneurs to cash in part of their equity.

Branson saw his opportunity to raise capital quickly to reduce the company's dependence on short-term bank borrowing and further expand without losing control of his company. (When the public company was eventually floated, Branson and his senior collaborators still controlled 63 percent of the voting stock.)

The flotation was not, in fact, the hasty decision it might have appeared to be. In anticipation of such an eventuality, Branson had made overtures to City institutions in 1985, raising £25 million for acquisitions in the form of preferred stock that, on conversion, gave holders a priority option to acquire equity in the company.

Much of the detail of this arrangement was handled by Don Cruickshank, appointed group managing director in 1984. A Scottish accountant with an MBA from Manchester Business School, Cruickshank had worked for McKinsey and in general management in the media industry. At ease in City circles, he was the kind of executive with whom bankers felt comfortable—an important factor in Branson's decision to recruit him. He complemented the skills and experience of the other long-serving executives: Draper; Ken Berry, the managing director of Virgin Records, who had started at Virgin as a junior accounts clerk; and Branson's brother-in-law, Robert Devereux, the Cambridge-educated head of what was then Virgin Vision. To strengthen financial management, in particular debt management and banking facilities, Cruickshank recruited Trevor Abbott, a trained accountant with ten years' management experience with the artist agency MAM, which smoothed his path into the new slot of group financial director since he was not seen as an outsider.

Cruickshank's primary task was to deconstruct the labyrinthine Virgin empire and create structure, systems, and organizational discipline with which the City would feel comfortable. It was immediately apparent that Virgin Atlantic and the other travel interests—which had yet to show a steady income—would not meet City expectations. These and peripheral interests such as the homosexual nightclub Heaven, were merged into a new private company, Voyager, to be owned by Branson and Draper. The remaining companies—Retail, Vision, and Music, together the largest and most profitable part by far of the Virgin Group—were prepared to be floated on the London stock exchange. The flotation was carried out successfully using the rather unusual method of offer-by-tender, whereby investors nominate a price that is then accepted or rejected. The striking price of 140p per share valued the public company at approximately £240 million. City institutions holding preferred stock took up their option to convert their holding to common stock.

Other institutions acquired part of the new issue through subscription and trading in the aftermarket created by profit taking among smaller shareholders, who initially numbered eighty-five thousand. Virgin artists and employees acquired 7 percent of the new issue under the terms of the offer, which gave them priority access to up to 10 percent.

Despite the demand for stock, the market flotation was not the success that Branson or the investors had expected. Although recording better-than-expected profits, Virgin's share price performed badly following the flotation and later fell precipitately when the London exchange crashed in October 1987. Moreover, relations between Virgin management and City analysts were at best uneasy. Branson was unsuited to cultivating the type of relationship that the chairman of a public company must have with institutional investors. Although he appreciated the discipline the public quotation had imposed on the company, nevertheless he felt the City undervalued Virgin and failed to understand the entrepreneurial nature of his business, especially the music division. The analysts in turn were uncomfortable with the vagaries of a business where most of the assets—rock musicians and their creative output—were valued against the ephemeral nature of current public taste. Their doubts and concerns were reinforced by the unpredictable nature of the chairman and the demands on his time from his publicity stunts, airline business, and charitable activities.

Unwilling to tolerate the constraints placed upon him but determined to help the many small investors who had seen the value of their investment diminish, Branson finally resolved to quit the stock market. In July 1988 he announced his decision to raise privately £200 million to be used to buy out the publicly held stock at the original asking price, in effect compensating the original shareholders who at that point faced a considerable paper loss. Richard Branson thus honored a moral debt he felt he owed and was once more master of his own destiny.

"TOO OLD TO ROCK, TOO YOUNG TO FLY"

With a major debt to repay and in need of a substantial capital injection to finance his ambitions for the company, Branson recognized that he still needed external investors. In light of his stock market experiences, however, this time he was more circumspect.

In the years following privatization, Branson was still an opportunistic, intuitive entrepreneur, but he followed a path of rationalization through joint ventures with established companies. This approach permitted his company to expand, both in terms of products and geography. The most significant deal was the sale of 25 percent of Virgin records to Fujisankei, Japan's largest media company, for £115 million. Another Japanese company—Seibu Saison, the hotel chain—paid £10 million for 10 percent of Voyager, which had recently acquired landing rights in Tokyo through Virgin Atlantic. He also gave minority shareholdings to talented managers. (In Virgin Communications, for example, about twenty managers have equity options; in Retail, a further twenty-five do.)

In the UK, Virgin's retail interests were consolidated around the Megastore concept in a joint venture with a major retailer.

Enjoying prestigious locations in major cities, Megastores sell home entertainment products—music, videos, and books—on a large scale. They replaced the string of small secondary retail outlets for which Virgin had become known. The success of the Megastore concept was exported to major cities throughout the world, frequently through joint ventures.

Virgin entered many deals of this kind as it adjusted to Branson's new direction, although Branson would probably have found it difficult to say precisely what that direction was. After turning forty, he experienced a period of introspection and self-doubt, becoming more reflective about his business and other interests. He had long ago left the management of the music company to Draper and Berry; Devereux was successfully running Virgin Communications with virtual autonomy, expanding its U.S. activities. The retail division had never held any particular attraction for Branson.

Only the airline gave him the sense of excitement and involvement he sought. Virgin Atlantic had advanced dramatically from the original low-cost, low-fare operation envisaged by Randolph Fields. It now competed with the major carriers, winning awards for service and plaudits from the vital customer segment of business travelers. But airlines are notoriously capital-intensive, and if Branson's target to fly to the world's twenty major cities were to be realized, more cash was needed.

By the early 1990s, Virgin Atlantic was a serious threat to the major airlines, none more so than British Airways (BA). The UK's national carrier was led by the ebullient and forthright Lord King. Despite the recession, the Gulf War, and increasingly ferocious competition, Virgin Atlantic was able to exploit the UK government's competition policy to expand its routes, winning vital landing rights at the expense of BA. But Virgin remained a relatively small player in the airline business, still vulnerable to the tactics that had pushed Laker into bankruptcy. To defend his position, Branson constantly lobbied politicians as well as European and U.S. officials, seeking assurances that unfair competition, however defined, would not be permitted.

He found politicking a tiring distraction from the main activity of getting people to fly Virgin Atlantic. The company had suffered financially, and Branson was reconciled to finding a major capital investment to ensure the airline's long-term future. Realistically, such capital could only come from the sale of the record business—the jewel in the Virgin crown, and the largest remaining independent record company in the world.

After long discussions with his immediate team, and a degree of soul searching, Branson entered into negotiations with Bertelsmann and Thorn EMI, realizing that he was currently in a strong enough position to achieve a sale on his own terms. Thorn's offer of cash or stock (Branson took the cash) to a value of £560 million won the day. Virgin Music, with tangible assets of £3 million, was sold in March 1992, creating a newly combined music business with 18 percent of the world market. City comments that Thorn had overpaid for Virgin were quickly discounted. Rationalization of Virgin staff and bands improved Thorn's profits by more than £80 million in 1993–94.

At the time of the sale, some Virgin Music employees felt misled by Branson. They assumed they were to share in the profits from the sale of the company. Branson had commanded great loyalty, providing opportunities for promotion (especially for women) that were unusual and generous for the industry. He encouraged them to dream and forget about commercial details. Now the employees were forced to admit that he had never made any concrete financial promises to them. Once again, he proved to be a brilliant leader who believes in putting employees first, but at the same time a tough negotiator who has learned that positive cash flow is essential to Virgin's interests.

Simon Draper, who for some time had been losing interest in day-to-day management of the business, joined the new owners but gradually reduced his involvement to pursue private interests; Ken Berry remains as managing director of Virgin Music. Many of the long-serving staff attended an emotional farewell party after which Branson said, "Too many entrepreneurs have gone down because they were not prepared to cash in their chips at the right time."

The battle between British Airways and Virgin Atlantic became increasingly acrimonious and personalized around its two leaders. Lord King was quoted as saying that Branson had discovered that he "was too old to rock, and too young to fly." Matters came to a head when a television program alleged BA's use of dirty tricks against Virgin Atlantic: breaking into its computer system to target its customers, spreading disinformation about Virgin's financial state, and diverting its customers at U.S. airports to BA flights. Branson immediately sued BA for damages, claiming £11 million. Lord King's denials were in terms that Branson found offensive. He sued King for libel and ultimately won substantial damages, humiliating the BA chairman and accelerating the latter's retirement after an otherwise distinguished business career.

The sale of the record company saw the departure of many long-serving staff. This, combined with evolutionary changes in retail, growth of the airline, and creation of new companies, moved Virgin away from its roots and previous management structure. The Virgin Group would now be overseen by a triumvirate: Richard Branson, Trevor Abbott, and Robert Devereux, each with his own interests and fiefdom. (Abbott remained active in this role until 1997, when, to pursue other interests, he became a nonexecutive director of the main Virgin holding company. He died unexpectedly in late 1997.)

Devereux ran Communications, now renamed Entertainment, at arm's length from the other activities in the group. This separation was justified by the operational approach, which is more akin to the former music division wherein a few people, through "innovation and intellectual power, add high value to a low capital base." With his staff, all of whom were recruited locally and scattered around the world (50 percent in the United States, 30 percent in the UK, 20 percent in France and Germany), Devereux insisted on a tight cash-management system and detailed budgets to keep him in touch—a common theme throughout Virgin, which has a sophisticated centralized data processing unit to maintain information flow.

At that time, Abbott was the self-acknowledged hatchet man at Virgin, putting the many ideas that surface into a structured form that could be integrated into the Virgin organization. He spent much of his time "creating business partnerships that equate to platonic marriages." Once a partnership was set up—with Virgin's interests tightly controlled—one of his managing directors would run the project. This management philosophy kept the organization flat. His financial watchwords were "build the balance sheet, watch the cash," an approach justified, he believed, by the fact that Virgin is privately owned and has no need to maximize profits in the short term.

Branson's main business interest was Virgin Atlantic, where he was frequently involved in much of the detail of the operation. His commitment to the airline was, and still is, total. (It is the only company of his group of which he remained managing director for a long time. In all other companies, he quickly assumed the more hands-off position of chairman.) He has even given his home phone number to all the airline's staff so they can call him with ideas, difficulties, and complaints; he follows up any proposal that gives the airline a competitive edge.

In large part because of Branson's drive and attention to detail, Virgin Atlantic has become an international leader in the small-airline class. Branson believes that Virgin can be both small and global, and he realizes that small airlines can and must compete on some basis other than price. This philosophy is reflected in Virgin's aggressive marketing style (one advertisement congratulated British Airways on lowering its fares to just $51 higher than Virgin's on one route) and emphasis on service and entertainment. From in-flight masseurs, tailors, and underwear fashion shows (with Branson himself as a model) to transportation to the airport in London on the back of a motorcycle, Virgin has been at the forefront of innovative service and entertainment since its inception. Branson says, "If you do something for fun and create the best possible product, then the profit will come." And it has. By 1988, it was Britain's number two long-haul carrier; Virgin Atlantic broke even in 1993 and has remained profitable ever since.

Branson has also expanded his airline in the European domestic market. His innovation here is to franchise Virgin's name to other airlines that agree to meet Virgin's standards, thereby increasing revenues for Virgin with no further investment and little risk. In early 1994, the first two franchises—London-Athens and London-Dublin—were established. The following year, a unique partnership was formed with Malaysia Airlines to operate to Kuala Lumpur and on to Australia; a European airline, Virgin Express, offered low-cost, no-frills service between Brussels and several European capitals.

As the franchise arrangement underscores, Virgin Atlantic has thrived because Branson is extremely cautious. For many years, he leased aircraft rather than buying them and avoided major acquisitions. He is fond of saying, "The quickest way to become a millionaire is to be a billionaire and buy an airline." Even so, Virgin Atlantic was the first customer for the new Airbus A340-600, unveiled at the Le Bourget air show in the summer of 1997; Virgin ordered sixteen customized craft to be delivered by the year 2002.

Branson's caution is also reflected in his belief in "creative adaptation." As creation of Virgin Atlantic itself proved, he does not hesitate to pick up an idea that has been pioneered by someone else. He has constantly battled any symptoms of the not-invented-here syndrome in his organization.

His other principal activity is promoting the Virgin name to potential partners, customers, and the world at large. Still impatient with traditional business practice, he rarely calls board meetings or has formal financial reviews, preferring to wait for problems to come to him for informal resolution with his senior collaborators. Always on the lookout for new opportunities, all he will say about the future is that he "[doesn't] want to run a conglomerate. People get lost and don't give their best. . . . I expect we will sell off parts of the business, maybe to managers. I am always open to suggestions." As ostensibly laid-back as this attitude appears, Branson keeps a firm hand on the controls of his company. In September 1997, Virgin announced the buyout of most of its joint-venture partners in the retail business, while simultaneously launching new retail ventures in clothing and cosmetics.

RICHARD BRANSON: A PORTRAIT

Family and Early Life

Richard Branson was born in July 1950, the first child and only son of Ted Branson and his wife, Eve, née Huntley-Flindt. He was later joined by two sisters, Lindi and Vanessa. The family has remained close, all enjoying what Richard was later to describe as a "happy and secure" childhood.

Both Ted and Eve came from comfortable establishment backgrounds. Ted was the son and grandson of eminent lawyers, a fact impressed on young Richard when he visited Madame Tussaud's Wax Museum in London with his father and saw models of murderers who were sentenced to hang by Sir George Branson, the boy's grandfather. Following family tradition, Ted left his Quaker-run school to study law at Cambridge University. After military service in World War II, he eventually qualified as a lawyer but, perhaps because of his Quaker education or his naturally kindly disposition, his career in advocacy (where adversarial skills are vital) was slow to get started.

Eve Huntley-Flindt came from a family of clerics, farmers, and stockbrokers, whose womenfolk were expected to have horizons beyond the home. While still a young girl, she trained as a dancer and appeared in London theaters, both in dance revues and as an actress. By the time she met Ted Branson she was a flight attendant, traveling to South America when air travel still held a significant element of adventure and danger. Determined, self-assured, and ambitious, at twenty-seven Eve was an attractive, outgoing young woman when she married Branson, the reserved and fair-minded young lawyer.

Eve had decided views on child rearing. She was never a martinet, but she pushed her children to be self-reliant and responsible, to take control of their own destiny rather than relying on others. One summer afternoon, as she and six-year-old Richard were on their way to visit his grandparents, Eve told Richard to get out of the car and try to find his own way. The farmhouse where they were staying was not far, but Richard got lost, ending up at the neighbor's farm. Eve now admits that she might have been overly enthusiastic about encouraging Richard's independence, but she has never regretted it. Clearly, Eve admired strength of character. She felt her children's ability to overcome challenges would encourage the kind of spirit she wanted to see in them. Accordingly, she used her own considerable energy to organize activities, games, and projects for her children that were not only fun but also served a useful purpose. Holidays, weekends, and other free time were used productively. The Branson household had no television, since it was deemed "time wasting"; shyness in children was simply bad manners and a self-indulgence to be discouraged; if money was short (as it was in the early days when Ted's father cut off his allowance in protest at his precipitate marriage), then a solution could always be found in small money-making schemes that Eve thought up. Bemoaning one's lot was never acceptable to her, and she lived up to her own standards.

Ted Branson was never a strict and remote father figure. Rather, he acted as a calm and considerate backstop to Eve's daily management of the children. Sympathetic and supportive by preference, a halfhearted disciplinarian if really necessary, he was less directly ambitious for his children than Eve, who expected, for example, that Richard would one day be prime minister.

Richard grew up to be the archetypal naughty boy. Frequently in minor scrapes, scolded for innumerable misdemeanors, and hyperactive in all he did, his parents found him both endearing and fatiguing. According to his father, he began his first business venture when he was around eleven or twelve years old. He planted a thousand seedlings and then went back to school convinced he would make a killing selling Christmas trees. Rabbits ate the trees. About a year, later he tried again. This time the scheme involved raising and selling budgerigars, a highly fecund small parrot. Another failure.

Richard's parents were particularly concerned about his progress at school, where his main accomplishments were on the sports field thanks to a strong physique and competitive spirit. His schoolboy heroes were sportsmen—particularly cricketers—and adventurers such as Robert Scott, the famous British explorer of the Antarctic and a distant relation by marriage. A serious leg injury, however, forestalled Richard's promising career in athletics, while a period of forced intensive study finally gained him admittance to Stowe school. His indifference to school work (not helped by long-undetected poor eyesight) continued, and he achieved only average results, which ruled out a legal or other professional career. By contrast, *Student* magazine excited Branson with its possibilities and offered a timely and convenient exit. So, with his parents' reluctant blessing (his father's support was particularly influential), he quit school.

Branson left few friends behind him. While not unpopular, his energetic and single-minded pursuit of what pleased him left little room for others. His indifference to the contemporary social mores and allegiances common in a school like Stowe left him somewhat isolated. His few friends were those inveigled into his various projects. Commenting on the end of his schooldays, Branson said that because he left school without getting a university degree, he decided to make money. He never considered the possibility of failure.

The "Hippie Entrepreneur"

Having in some respects commercialized the antiestablishment lifestyle of the 1960s, it was not surprising that Branson was labeled "the hippie entrepreneur" by the business and music press alike. His alternative image was reinforced by the company's operating style, where, from the start, informality and equality were essential principles—rarely found in the business world at the time.

When Virgin started out, everyone received the same low salary, there was no hierarchy (Branson was, and is, "Richard" to everyone), and personal attire was casual to the point of idiosyncrasy. Even after the company expanded massively, this style was very much in evidence: Branson and staff are rarely seen in conventional business clothes, preferring sweaters and jeans even on formal occasions. Similarly, the company's offices, accumulated over time, were a collection of modest and often dilapidated buildings scattered about northwest London from which the sound of rock music could usually be heard.

For a long time, Branson's office and home was a canal houseboat, where he worked alone except for the presence of two secretaries. One bedroom acted as the office, while Branson operated from a dining table in the small sitting room. On occasion, it is reported, the bathroom served as the boardroom—with Branson conducting meetings from his bath. Eventually, he was forced to move to a larger home, since his two children were starting to answer the phones, but he kept the houseboat as an office.

His wife, a down-to-earth Glaswegian from a working-class background, has no interest or role in his business life. This is something of an anomaly at Virgin since Branson, contrary to conventional wisdom, is a great believer in working with family and friends, seeing only the advantages and not the risks. His cousins, aunts, school and childhood friends, parents, and former girlfriends have all been drawn into his various business activities. Only his first wife found the situation difficult to accept, but even she is now in a joint venture with Branson, developing hotels in Spain. The charges of nepotism that such arrangements usually engender were muted at Virgin because Branson adopted a promote-from-within policy, giving many of his staff opportunities that their lack of experience and training would preclude in more conventional companies. Virgin was unconventional in other ways, too. Somehow, Branson created the impression that people worked at Virgin for fun and excitement rather than simply as a means of earning a living. Notoriously indifferent to material possessions and unconcerned about everyday financial matters, Branson saw no difficulty in paying modest salaries provided people were enjoying themselves, feeling part of an idiosyncratic enterprise that had a heart. If people were down, a party would revive spirits—and, incidentally, give Branson a chance to play a practical joke on newcomers, an embarrassing rite of passage at Virgin that is maintained to this day.

Much of this operating style was established not so much by design but by the exigencies of the time when Virgin was getting started. It has proved to be a successful model that Branson can replicate. His philosophy is to immerse himself in a new venture until he understands the ins and outs of the business, and then hand it over to a good managing director and financial controller, who are given a stake in it and then expected to make the company take off. He knows that expansion through creation of additional discrete legal entities not only protects the Virgin Group but also gives people a sense of involvement and loyalty, particularly if he trusts them with full authority and offers minority shareholding to the managers of subsidiaries. He is proud of the fact that Virgin has produced a considerable number of millionaires. He has said that he does not want his best people to leave the company to start a venture outside; he prefers to make millionaires within.

His use of joint ventures is an extension of this model and is reinforced by his dealings with the Japanese. Branson is impressed by the Japanese approach to business, admiring their commitment to the long term and how they take time to build a business through organic growth rather than acquisitions. (He proudly states that he has purchased only one major company, Rushes Video, for £6 million some years ago.) He sees similarities in the Japanese *keiretsu* system (small companies interlocking in a collaborative network) to the structure he has created at Virgin, with more than five hundred small companies around the world operating quasi-independently.

"Seven Minutes to Go . . . I Just Want to Get out of This"

In January 1997, Richard Branson was in Morocco, poised to embark on the latest in a series of personal challenges: this time, a race to circumnavigate the world by hot air balloon. Of the three balloons taking part, the Virgin Global Challenger, piloted by a Swede, Per Lindstrand, was the most technically sophisticated. According to a joke circulating in the simmering excitement preceding the launch, it required a crew of three, two men and a dog: Lindstrand to fly the balloon, Branson to feed the dog, and the dog to bite Branson if he got near the controls. They *were* three, the third being a man named Alex Ritchie, a last-minute stand-in for one of the original crew members who fell ill. In a blaze of publicity, which nevertheless poignantly saw Branson's family in tears, the balloon rose in the air. Disaster struck almost immediately. In their haste to get the balloon airborne, the ground crew had forgotten to unlock the couplings on the fuel lines. This meant that, should the crew need to lose ballast fast, they would be unable to jettison the heaviest and most obvious weights: the fuel tanks attached to the capsule. The crew began to plan how they would unlock the couplings, but before they could do so, the balloon was caught by violent winds in its natural descent at sunset and began to plummet toward the ground. They threw out everything they could lift to try to slow the descent, but all attempts failed. Alex Ritchie then put on a parachute, climbed out onto the roof of the capsule, and opened two couplings. Seemingly seconds before they would hit the ground, they were able to drop a fuel tank and the balloon soared again. The crew landed in the Algerian desert the following morning. The flight lasted just twenty hours.

The venture was at the time the latest in a series of Branson exploits that began in 1985 when he attempted to cross the Atlantic in a high-powered speedboat to win the coveted Blue Riband, the prize awarded to the vessel and crew with the fastest time. The vessel sank off Ireland, but a second attempt the following year was successful. In 1987, he and Per Lindstrand attempted the fastest transatlantic balloon crossing, an aim achieved only after both barely escaped with their lives when the balloon made a forced landing in the Irish Sea. In 1990, Branson found himself in northern Japan preparing for takeoff in an attempt to make the first ever transpacific crossing in a hot air balloon, an event timed to coincide with Virgin Atlantic's inaugural flight to Tokyo. His Japanese hosts had invited a huge crowd to witness the event, with banners declaring him to be the "Hero of the World."

Branson is happy to admit that these exploits started as an inexpensive way of publicizing Virgin Atlantic, but with time they seemed to gain a momentum of their own. Asked how the chairman of a major corporation can justify the risks and expense, he replies, "People who have to ask the question don't understand." As their balloon was hurtling toward the African desert beneath them, he wrote in his log: "Seven minutes to go. . . . The dream is over. I just want to live. . . . I have cheated death 11 times. My life no longer flashes before me. I just want to get out of this." Forty-eight hours afterwards, despite the fear and panic and the tears and opposition of his family, Branson and Lindstrand were on a plane heading home and discussing their next adventure. In December 1997, a new attempt to circumnavigate the world was aborted as the balloon that was to be used for the venture was blown away by itself. In spite of this setback, the last word is not yet said about this adventure. Knowing Branson's persistence and competitiveness, one can bet he is not going to give up easily.

There is one member of his family who readily understands his motives. Before the ill-fated Virgin Global Challenger lifted off, Eve Branson handed her son a letter to be opened six days into the flight. A surprised Richard noted in his diary, "She is being sentimental at last." The letter was forgotten in the drama that followed, but he remembered it during his flight home and recorded: "I look forward to a rare outpouring of sentimentality. Alex [Ritchie] feels I should read it in private and moves to the other end of the plane. It begins: 'Dear Ricky, I have found this great estate in South Africa which I think you should look at.' She went on, for ten pages. I laughed all the way home."[2]

Whatever his motives, Branson has come to be seen as a modern buccaneer with an attractive, devil-may-care attitude about both physical danger and business risk. At the same time, he supports charitable, radical, and humanitarian causes. For example, he still funds a sex counseling clinic that he founded in his *Student* days when his girlfriend became pregnant and they had nowhere to turn to for advice. He also launched a new brand of condoms,

Mates, as a response to the government's laissez-faire attitude toward AIDS and condom use. This was the kind of project that appealed to him; it would do good for society and raise money for charity, and he would have fun doing it. More controversially, he boycotted a magazine that refused to carry ads supporting legalization of marijuana, although he personally dislikes illegal drugs (having once haplessly experimented with LSD; his girlfriend at the time said he could not stand to be out of control).

Branson's exploits and causes are diverse, ranging from a health care foundation supporting AIDS research to financial support for a new political publication. He used his aircraft to rescue people trapped by the Gulf War, and led an initiative to help unemployed teenagers. His anger and disappointment at failing to win the franchise for the British national lottery (his consortium planned to donate all proceeds to charity, unlike the proposal of the winning bidder) were difficult to surmount, and for a while he threatened the Office of the National Lottery with a judicial review of its decision. His commitment to such altruistic causes is as great as his commitment to his business affairs. He puts as much time and energy into a charitable foundation he is involved in as he does into the launch of a commercial enterprise such as Virgin Cola.

Branson's esteem in UK public opinion is regularly demonstrated. He was the darling of the former prime minister, Margaret Thatcher, although he has remained apolitical. He has been nominated for awards for enterprise, has been voted the nation's most popular businessman, and in general is the point of reference whenever comparisons are made between the traditional business leader and emerging entrepreneurs of the 1980s and 1990s. He is, however, a man of contrasts. The public persona is that of a warm, friendly, idealistic, family man. At the same time, he is highly competitive and a workaholic, and an extremely tough negotiator who thrives on bargaining.

The Real Richard Branson

Richard Branson has become an international celebrity; in the UK he is almost a folk hero. He recently ranked as the eleventh wealthiest person in the UK, with an estimated net worth of £895 million.

Asked to explain the strategy that got him to this point, he talks of minimizing risks—protect the downside, always be ready to walk away—and seeking opportunities to build the largest entertainment group outside the United States. Over the years, he has made a few strategic statements that, in hindsight, do not relate very much to subsequent events. Most frequently, however, he says he simply wants to enjoy himself.

But can a strategy for fun really explain creation of a music company by a founder who, paradoxically, has little interest in or knowledge of music? Equally, it is difficult to explain how a shy man, ill at ease when speaking publicly or in private conversation with strangers, can become a supreme self-publicist? How an establishment-born figure with intrinsically conventional views can become the champion of radical and libertarian causes? Or how the man who is almost obsessive about fair play can negotiate ferociously for the last penny in a deal? Will the real Richard Branson please stand up?

Obviously, the key to the success of the real Branson is found in his family background. We mentioned in Chapter One that the family is the first model of organization that we encounter. Branson's mother encouraged her son's self-reliance and competitiveness, convincing him that he would be able to do whatever he set his mind to. She not only taught him the value of money but also was the family's role model for entrepreneurship. Richard has said that she was the one "who would come up with one mad idea after another" to help out in times when, in the early days, the family's financial situation was precarious. Branson learned at a young age how to haggle and make deals, a talent that would serve him in good stead in many of his later business transactions.

We can assume that Branson's script in his inner theater was reinforced by his father's experience of being forced into a career as a barrister by his own father, who also opposed Ted Branson's decision to marry before finishing his studies. The career of this powerful and influential grandfather, Sir George Branson, a high court judge, must have had an effect on the fantasy life of young Richard; those visits to the waxworks evocations of his grandfather's reputation may have nourished in him a wish to become so successful and powerful himself. To add to this inner imagery, there was Scott of the Antarctic, whose exploits had made him a legendary hero to the British generally and even more so personally to Richard, given the family connection.

Branson's particular family constellation may explain to some extent his willingness to take up any dare. Continuing challenge seems to make him feel alive. His parents also believed in looking out for the underdog (recall the role model of Sir George Branson). As a result, Richard seems to be particularly willing to take on strong opponents if he sees a chance to put the world to rights. The David and Goliath theme appears to be a pattern running through his life; it may explain his involvement in social causes. Finally, his family experience undoubtedly encouraged his playfulness. Branson is a prankster, with a good sense of humor and, as has been emphasized before, a strong desire to have fun.

The core themes in his internal theater likely have something to do with being an explorer, taking people on adventures, doing your own thing, remaining independent, being daring—that is, controlling your own destiny, and challenging the establishment. His mother's influence has been substantial as an independent and daring person in her own right.

Thus, in the context of formative experiences, his exploits become less mysterious. The pieces of the puzzle that is Branson fall together if we consider the central themes of his internal theater. Applying this sort of insight helps us in general to deconstruct person-organization interfaces—that is, to understand how personality affects leadership style, and how the latter determines an organization's architecture.

CHAPTER THREE

An Interview with Richard Branson

When you meet Richard Branson in person,[1] your first impression is of a rather shy, unassertive individual—ironic in a person who is a master of the media, always prepared to come up with a new, daring proposition. Though communication is one of Virgin's core businesses, Branson can, at times, be quite inarticulate. He also has a very boyish appearance; journalists compare him to Peter Pan. At the same time, he also comes across as a warm, relaxed, considerate person. He makes a great effort to put others at ease; he has a winning smile. His style of dress helps break the ice; it is certainly a far cry from the sensible-suited "uniform" of most businessmen. Instead, there is the sweater and the casual trousers, not to mention the beard.

Branson is, above all, immensely likable. He is the kind of person with whom you would like to spend more time or embark on an adventure. Behind this public persona of a relaxed family man, however, is an extremely competitive workaholic who can be very shrewd in his dealings with others.

His lack of pomposity, quite uncommon among business leaders, helps to put others at ease. Given his charm, one quickly recognizes why Branson has been so successful in dealing with people and inspiring his employees. He seems to avoid the pitfalls of his position and retain a sense of modesty. Many executives would have a hard time coping with the fame he has achieved; such an experience could become too heady, with unfortunate repercussions for both the person and the company.

Branson is never dogmatic; in fact, he often speaks hesitantly. He is not given to monologues. He has taught himself to be a good listener, and he is willing to change his mind if an argument is convincing. At the same time, he does not give the impression of being a navel gazer. On the contrary, he is very action oriented. Notwithstanding a strong pragmatic side to his way of thinking, he shows a certain playfulness in his behavior, a quality that brings out the best in people.

When you look at your career, what do you see as the critical decision points? How do you feel about the choices you have made over the years?

Well, obviously, I suppose the first one was deciding to leave school at a young age. I started this magazine at school. The aim of it was to give young people a voice, to put the world right. At the time, the headmaster gave me a choice: either you do your education or you do your magazine. You can't do both. I decided to leave school to run the magazine. Obviously, that was a critical decision point. The magazine turned out to be my form of management education. I spent four or five years running it, going out and doing interviews, meeting people, learning from those interviews, and perhaps most importantly, learning the art of survival. I had to sell enough advertising to pay the bills to cover the printing and paper cost, and sort out the distribution. I needed to have a table big enough to dive under when somebody came to collect the bills that hadn't been paid. I had to juggle all the time and learn how to survive; that was the first really critical decision.

From then on, things just evolved. Never was there any sort of mapping things out five years ahead. Perhaps I should have done that, but I never did. Then one day somebody turned up who loved music. He was a cousin of mine from South Africa, Simon Draper. He bought around a thousand records from our little Virgin mail order company. So I thought, maybe we should consider setting up a record company. Coincidentally, around the same time Mike Oldfield turned up with a tape, *Tubular Bells,* which we liked very much. That was another critical stage. The next step, I suppose, if one really looks back, was building up the retail shops.

Actually, a *lot* of companies evolved out of the record company. If you had a record company, you needed shops to sell your products; you needed an export company to export your records; you needed foreign companies to distribute records abroad and market them well; you needed editing suites to edit film video; and so on.

We decided to create companies which would stand on their own, companies in themselves. Looking back, I suspect the biggest difference between us and other independent record companies was that we decided to set up our own companies around the world ourselves rather than giving the rights for our products to other people. Suddenly, we had substantial companies in Germany and France. Japan and America were also signing on local bands as well.

Then I suppose the next really radical step took place in 1984: going into the airline business. It was a move that everybody thought was mad, looking at it in purely economic terms. And the critics included my closest friends. It was a business, however, where I felt we could bring something that others could not bring. I mean, in 1984 the airlines were all run abysmally. Their way of doing business was really terrible. As far as service quality was concerned, the airline business was perhaps the worst run of almost any business I can think of. The big airlines tried to get away with as much as they could. They were either national airlines or just ex-national airlines. They charged as much as they could. Their costs had gone through the roof. They offered the customers the minimum because they could afford to do so, being monopolies or duopolies. We decided to try to get in there and compete and offer really good-quality service. Looking back at that decision, the past ten years have been very exhilarating, great fun.

There is this saying: "The best way to become a millionaire is to start off as a billionaire and go into the airline business!" Obviously, I have been very aware of that observation and have tried to avoid it ever coming about. There have been major moments in that last ten years, in particular when British Airways decided that we had become a threat that was likely to get out of control. They decided to use the most unbelievable tactics to put us out of business. I must admit, one of the most delightful moments of my life was winning the British Airways dirty-tricks court case. Winning that particular battle, winning that court case, meant in a sense that Virgin had come into its own. At that point, companies such as Boeing and Airbus and others, who used to be frightened to do business with us because we had the might of British Airways attempting to put us out of business, began to change their minds.

They decided to deal with us when they realized that we could take on British Airways and beat them. I think they also realized that it was unlikely that BA would try the same tactics again. There we go: life history!

What do you see as Virgin's key success factors? What makes your company different from others?

I'm absolutely certain that it is a question of the kind of people you have, the way you motivate them. I'm sure that is what can make any company successful. If you can motivate your people, you can get through bad times and you can enjoy the good times together. If you fail to motivate your people, your company is doomed not to perform well.

I find that I spend a lot of time trying to concentrate on motivating people. For instance, once a week I will go down to the airline to give fifty new employees their wings or, if they are joining the reservations group, something else, to make sure that I see everybody who joins us at least once. If the cabin crew joins a company like Virgin, they join for the romance, for the flying. Yet, with most airlines, they soon realize that there is no romance in flying. What we try to do is to make sure that there is. Thus, the kinds of hotels where they stay are nice hotels, not airport hotels, hotels with swimming pools and pleasant environments. It also comes down to making sure that all these little things are sorted out with your staff, that you don't go and make crass decisions which upset all of the people working for the company. If your staff is happy and smiling and enjoying their work, they will perform well. Consequently, the customers will enjoy their experience with your company. If your staff is sad and miserable and not having a good time, the customers will be equally miserable. So it is a critical thing.

I am, for example, proud that I get lots of lovely comments and letters about the fact that we have created what may be one of the best airlines in the world. I go to great lengths to be in touch with the staff. I write them a letter once every month. In that letter, I give them lots of chatty details about what we are planning to do, what's going on. The key is that in the end of the letter, I will always say "This is my home address, this my home telephone number. If you have any suggestions, any problems, any ideas, just write me a letter." On average, I get maybe fifteen or sixteen letters a day from members of the staff. In a sense, that is not so many. And in a sense, it is quite easy for me to deal with. I always make sure that my staff letters are the first letters to be answered. Within the letters, some superb ideas come up, and also some bad decisions that have been made. I can find out about them within twenty-four hours, and I can deal with them. One or two staff members might even be writing about personal things having to do with themselves. That's fine as well. I personally believe that if each chairman of every company were to communicate directly to every staff member and get them to write about their problems, the need for trade unions would be that much less. If communication would go directly from the bottom to the top, the company would be run that much better as a result.

Part of Virgin's management philosophy is based on the fundamental belief that the individual is all-important in our company. And in some ways, I place more importance on the junior people in my companies than I do on the senior people. I do get quite angry when senior people come in saying that they want another thirty thousand pounds, or whatever, while at the same time they are asking their junior people to tighten their belts. Basically, I am trying to ensure that we hire people who are good with people. Given the way we value our people at Virgin, we will very rarely fire anybody. To do that kind of thing is very demoralizing for everybody.

Could you say something about how you design your organization—its architecture?

Well, our record company [now divested], I suppose, would have been the best example. My philosophy was always that if there were fifty people in a building I would go there and ask to see the deputy managing director, the deputy sales manager, the deputy marketing manager, the deputy press officer. I would say: "You are now the managing director, the sales manager, the marketing manager, or the press officer of a new company." I would put them into a new building. Then again, when that company got to a certain size—fifty people—I would do the same thing again. So we actually set up about twenty-five or thirty small record companies.

Cumulatively, they became the biggest independent record company in the world. And they never lost major artists. Major artists stayed with them because they would identify with the small teams. Also, if you're given a card by somebody who says he is the managing director you might, I am afraid, take him more seriously than if you were given a card saying that the person was the deputy to the deputy to the deputy to the deputy managing director.

I think an important thing was learning the art of delegation at a very young age. I just didn't have enough hours in the day to do otherwise. Early on I decided to set up companies, immerse myself 100 percent in them, learn all about them—the airline is a good example—appoint a managing director and a very good senior accountant, and then let the managing director assume authority for the day-to-day problems. I can then spend my time instigating new ventures for the Virgin group. . . . I think it is obviously very important that you motivate people and draw out the best in them, and not assume that everyone is going to do everything exactly as you would do it. Sometimes they'll do it better; sometimes they won't do it as well. You have to accept things being done differently; this is one of the first things you have got to do if you are a good delegator.

For some things, maybe not directly but more subtly, don't you think you give your people specific directions?

I don't, actually. What I do is I employ, and I promote the kind of people who I can see are good at motivating people and are good leaders. We like each other, and we respect each other's good and bad points. I sometimes think it is more important to have somebody who is a good motivator of people rather than just a good businessman, so we look for people with good personalities—people who will put people who are working for them first, rather than themselves.

How do you find out if something is going wrong in your very diverse organization? What kind of information is essential to you?

We have a head office with a financial director for the group, which receives the accounts and keeps an eye on cash flow. But to a large extent, the individual companies get on and run their units by themselves.

Really, I don't look regularly at the information. I guess, Trevor Abbott looks at the figures on a more frequent basis. The exception to that rule is with one company: that's the travel group, for which I am now managing director as well as chairman. Therefore, I am much more involved in the day-to-day running of that group.

In 99 percent of the companies, I have appointed managing directors who are really running those companies. They have a stake in those companies. I have to find out very little, except what those managing directors tell me on occasion.

When you look at high-performance organizations, they seem to have a number of characteristics. They tend to have extremely visionary, enthusiastic leadership. They value their people and spend a lot of time training them. They are very entrepreneurial, with entrepreneurship pushed deep down in the organization. They are performance-driven, with high accountability. Their organizational design tends to be simple since the structure of the organization is not very complicated. And they know the competitive advantage of speed. Do you have any comments to make about how Virgin fits into that particular framework?

Well, I like to think that we fit into most of those categories. Obviously, speed is something which we are better at than most other companies. I mean, we don't have formal board meetings, committees, etc. If someone has an idea, they can pick up the phone and talk to me. I can vote "Done, let's do it." Or better still, they can just go ahead and do it. They know that they are not going to get a mouthful from me if they make a mistake. Analyzing things to death is not our kind of thing. We very rarely sit back and analyze what we do.

What can you say about your reward systems? You once said that you were in the business of making millionaires.

Yes, I suppose that we have made maybe fifteen or twenty multi-millionaires through this structure. In the last two years, we have also paid out over £150 million pounds to people whom we have given stakes in companies to. I think, however, as a private company it is more difficult to bring in schemes to involve everybody in the same way you can with a public company, where you have shares. But that is something which I think in the future we have got to try to address. We have to make sure that it is not just part of the wage package. There is a danger in doing so. At the moment, we tend to reward our people more in a paternalistic way. If somebody has performed really well, we all sing from the mountain and thank them the best we can. But we need to formalize that a bit in the future.

What do you see as your weaknesses? Do you have any characteristics that get in the way of your work?

I suspect not being able to say no. Hopefully, I am getting better at it now. But there are so many wonderful ideas. And I do love new projects; I love new ideas. We are in a position where almost any-body and everybody who has got an idea loves to bring it to us. There aren't many companies like us, who have got, in a sense, a certain amount of entrepreneurial flair, companies which seem accessible to the public. Therefore, in any one day we receive hun-dreds of requests of all sorts. And some of them are very good ones.

My weaknesses really go back to the fact that I have spread myself too thin. In a purely business sense, I suspect if I wanted just to maximize profits I should have stayed more focused on one area and really concentrated on that one area. That's the most con-ventional way, which I'm sure most business schools teach. Perhaps it is right. Having said so, it wouldn't have been half as much fun. I wouldn't have gotten half as much enjoyment out of life. I have no regrets at all in trying to break the mold and taking a different approach. That different approach has resulted in Virgin, as a brand name, being one of the best-known brand names in the world. It is a brand name which is well respected.

As a matter of fact, we actually have started companies just because of the name. For example, we started a skiing company called Virgin Snow just because the name was so delightful. The same is true for Virgin Water, Virgin Cola, and Virgin Bride, because these seemed such great names. The other reason that drives us to start something new is when we feel that something hasn't been done very well by other people; we can do it better.

The importance of having a name like Virgin for the company cannot be overemphasized. Over the next twenty years, we can use that brand name to break into a number of different areas and hopefully create a number of other quite successful companies.

But in spite of all these new ideas flowing in, we do make an effort to be firmer, to say no, simply because we don't have the time to concentrate on what we have already taken on.

As an aside, my wife says my biggest weaknesses are sticky pudding and pretty women.

What has been your biggest disappointment? Are there any regrets?

I have never looked back. I always like to look forward. But when all is said and done, I never thought that I would sell anything. The trouble with selling something is that you are selling people as well. I think that when we sold the record company, we cut off a limb or two from our own body. However much I can justify the reasons for it, it is sad that it has happened. I think it was a necessity. It was important that we did it, for the staff of Virgin Records plus the staff of all the other companies, plus the new companies that we now could start given the billion dollars we got for it. But it still is nasty, a limb chopped off. After all those years together, it was a pity to have to do it.

Some people argue that you run your company almost like a venture capital firm. Basically, anybody with a crazy idea gets a hearing.

I hope that "crazy idea" part is not too true. But to an extent, that statement is valid. I think that is a fair comment.

One way of making these crazy ideas come true is through your partnership arrangements. Could you say something about that?

Well, as a private company, one way of expanding is to bring in partners rather than to go to the City and bring in outside shareholders. One of the advantages of bringing in partners rather than small shareholders is that you can *choose* partners. Both parties also bring something to the table. In Japan, we have a company called Marui who are partners with us on a retail operation. Marui is also one of the biggest retailers in Japan. So we have the advantage that they fund the expansion of Virgin Retail in Japan, and they also have a great deal of retail expertise. Virgin brings the Virgin brand name and retail expertise in record retailing. It has been extremely successful.

What do you look for in partners?

Basically, we are looking for people we respect as far as the businesses they have built up to date—individuals that we like.

Many of your partnerships, I understand, are on a fifty-fifty basis, which means the key word is trust.

Yes, it is like a marriage. We have American partners as well. For example, there is Blockbuster [Video] in America. Interestingly enough, both sets of marriages—American and Japanese—have been very amiable. However, I do remember that a Japanese chairman of a major record company, Fujisankei—who wanted to buy a stake in our record company some years ago—came to me. We were being courted by an American company at the same time. We had to make up our minds the next day. He said, over dinner, "Would you rather be married to a Japanese wife or an American wife?" I think what he was trying to say was that a Japanese partner would interfere far less than an American partner.

So you married a Japanese partner?

Yes, we did.

Some people have said that your style has an exhibitionist quality. They wonder if other people in Virgin could be in the limelight. They mention that some of your stronger executives have left the company.

As far as public limelight is concerned, I think that a chairman of a company, of certain kind of company, should use himself to promote his company. Up until 1984, we didn't have any companies that needed the name promoted. We had things like record companies, studios, and the like, which really didn't need a high public profile. When we launched the airline, however, we needed a company which had a high public profile. After having talked to Freddy Laker, I decided that I would use myself to get out and promote the airline.

I used to find that I was extremely uncomfortable in front of the camera. I had to slightly force myself, initially. Somebody once told me that the best way of dealing with being in front of a camera is just to pretend that you are sitting in your living room talking to a friend. That comment has helped me a great deal.

I think that if I invite you to my home for a party, and if I stand in the corner and I'm reserved, all dressed up in my suit sipping sherry, everybody in that room is going to find that party pretty dull. If the chairman of the company is out there having a good time and he's the first person willing to get in the swimming pool, then everybody will be in the pool; everybody will have a good time.

It's critical that the top person enjoy himself. If you have a company which is run by somebody who's dull and not having a good time, then somehow it just permeates the whole way down. A company, to a large extent, either reflects the very top person or reflects all the top people who are running the company.

As a leader, it is extremely important that you are willing to be open and get out there, talk to the press, and give them a good time, make sure that they have the photographs they want so that your story ends up in the front pages rather than the back pages. That is something which I have learned. I think this way of doing things has been important for Virgin.

What about the other comment: that some of the stronger people, like Don Cruickshank or Nik Powell, have left your organization?

Well, I think that if you actually look at Virgin's history, you will find that its strength has been the fact that by far the majority of people have stayed with Virgin for a long time. It is very rare to find this kind of record in other companies or the government. It has been a tremendous strength. And even after these people leave, we will be friends for the rest of our lives. Don Cruickshank joined us to bring the company public. When the company went private again, he didn't see a role for himself.

As far as Nik Powell is concerned, we were friends when we were two years old. We stayed together until we were thirty years old, and we split amicably. Nik, Simon, and Ken [Simon Draper and Ken Barry, who were senior executives in the music company, which was sold in 1992] and others were in a sense more appropriate for the company at a certain point in time. It is like a marriage. It is supposed to last forever, but sometimes it doesn't work out that way.

What is good at twenty may not be good at forty.

The actual parting leaves the two halves stronger, rather than being forced [to stay] together.

Some of the top executives I have met, when they become well known, go off the deep end; they can't handle the power and the fame that comes with the job. What is your recipe? How do you manage it?

Well, I think the main thing I have tried to do is to keep my private life separate from my public life. So, for instance, my wife: you will almost never read an interview with her or see any articles about her. We have kept the kids completely out of the press as well. Basically, I will use myself to do interviews about my businesses but will never use myself to do interviews about my private life. I think as long as you can keep the two divorced, you can lead a private life and not let that interfere with your public life. It is my way of not letting the public criticisms or praise make my head get too big or too small.

Somehow, in many of your dealings you have played the role of David fighting a Goliath, identifying with the underdog. It seems to be a real pattern going through your life.

Remember, our general policy has almost always been never to buy companies. We have always *built* companies. So we have always been a small person taking on a big person. When we started Retail, we were the first people who discounted records against the big retailers who were selling records at full price. That was the way that we moved into that market. When we launched our Mates condom company, Durex had a 98 percent monopoly. We were trying to break a monopoly. With the airline, it was the same thing. We started with one plane, taking on British Airways, which was obviously extremely well established. Likewise, obviously, going into the cola market, taking on Coca Cola, again a brand name which is the biggest brand in the world. It will be an exciting challenge.

It is a tremendous challenge just to try to survive. Throughout my whole life, in every business I been in, the word *survival* has been the critical word. I am very naughty. At times when I could [instead choose to] live happily ever after, I will throw my life and my family and my business partners into turmoil by getting into another survival battle.

Some people actually say about you that you must have a death wish.

I definitely don't have a death wish, you know. But I have come close to death on a number of occasions and haven't enjoyed the experience at all. The ballooning trip across the Pacific: I had forty hours in which I didn't think I was going to come home. We had lost some fuel tanks, and many other things had gone wrong. It wasn't a pleasant feeling at all. The exhilaration when we actually did come home, when we succeeded, I guess, made me forget some of the worst, nightmarish moments. But I do love a challenge.

Talking about risky things, I also once ended up flying a plane which took off by mistake, having not learned how to fly it on my own. I once ended up pulling the cord which got rid of the parachute, rather than the cord that opened the parachute! So I think that I have used up about eight of my nine lives, which is one of the reasons that I am behaving myself a bit more now. Obviously, in a business sense the riskiest move I have made, I suppose, is starting the airline.

I must admit that I feel very much alive when I set out to achieve something. On reflection, it's really more the fighting than the actual achieving. I love people, and I just love new challenges. Some people say, "Why keep battling on when you can take it easy?" My reason, basically, is that I'm very fortunate to be in this position at my age. I've learned a great deal, and I've had great fun doing so. I'm in a unique position of being able to do almost anything I like and achieve almost anything I wish. I don't want to waste the position that I find myself in. I know that at age eighty or ninety, I would kick myself if I just frittered away this second half of my life. I really do believe that fighting competition is exciting. And it's good for business. I think that Virgin can get in there, and it can compete with the biggest and improve them. And hopefully survive alongside them, and pay the bills at the same time.

Basically, I admire anyone that takes on either the establishment or something like a mountain and succeeds or fails. As a matter of fact, anyone who tries to do the impossible. I admire just as much someone like Freddy Laker as somebody else who has actually succeeded.

It is, however, a fact that most entrepreneurs fail sometime in life. It is extremely rare to follow an entrepreneur's career for forty years and find that they have not failed at some stage.

What gets you angry?

I very rarely get angry; I think it's so counterproductive to get angry. If somebody really messed us up badly, I wouldn't say anything. I'd just maybe quietly not deal with that person again in the future. Even then, I'm apt to give somebody a second and a third and a fourth chance, because I know my own vulnerabilities. I know how easy it is to mess up in life. I think people are apt to judge people far too quickly.

Can you say something about your personal background?

I have been very fortunate that I have come from a very stable environment, a very happy, loving, supportive background. My parents have equally wanted me to stand on my own two feet. They have gone out of their way to do so. I have also two wonderful younger sisters.

It is interesting to note that you come from a family of barristers. Your grandfather was actually a judge on the High Court. In contrast, you became an entrepreneur. Your mother seems to have been the entrepreneur in the family.

Yes, my parents are opposites. My mother is extremely entrepreneurially minded. She never sits still. She is always coming up with another mad idea, a new project. She helped to keep us fed as children by making and selling table mats and tissue boxes and these kinds of things. She has always had some new project on the go and would never allow us to watch television or watch football matches. We always had to be out there doing things, playing football, being on the other side of the television set. My father, on the other hand, has always been quite laid back and very loving. I must admit that, if I ring up, I always ask for dad first. He is much more the opposite: he is somebody that is very easygoing, very unambitious, who has a great sense of humor.

What is your earliest memory?

My earliest memory was of an old bumpity-bump car. The memory is of my dad carrying us from the car, patting us on the back, telling us not to wake up. My parents always used to be there; a baby sitter was nonexistent. We used to sleep in the back of this bumpity-bump car wherever they went. It was always a nice, soothing feeling, your dad telling you not to wake up.

One of the reasons that I asked you this question is a story going around about you that perhaps illustrates your self-sufficiency. It has to do with finding your way back home at a very early age. Do you remember that incident?

I remember it well. I doubt whether parents would be able to do that to their children in this day and age. I must have been around six. We were in the countryside, visiting my grandparents. We were driving to see them in our car. There were only a few fields to go. My mother shoved me out of the door at about six at night and said "Right, make your own way back." I got lost. It got darker and darker. My poor parents got more and more panicky and obviously realized that this time they may have gone one step too far. I ended up at a neighboring farmhouse. I think maybe I even quite enjoyed the thrill of it by the time I got to the farmhouse.

Your move into the airline business was perhaps predetermined. It was a highly unusual move, given the portfolio of companies you had at that time. I remember that I asked you, years ago, whether you had ever read the management best-seller In Search of Excellence *[by Tom Peters and Robert Waterman]. Your answer was, "No, I didn't read it, I bought the book, like 90 percent of the population." I mentioned at the time that your company possessed most of the excellent qualities described in that book, except the criterion of sticking to the things you are good at. Of course, I was referring to the airline at the time. When I said that, you smiled, walked out of the room, and came back with a picture. You showed me a photograph of a stewardess dressed in an old-fashioned BA uniform. Underneath was written, "From an old virgin to a new Virgin, love, your mother." I wonder to what extent your mother's adventures as a stewardess—being one of the first to fly over the Andes—made you so interested in the airline business, even to the extent that it is the only company where you have retained the title of managing director. Is there some truth in this observation, or is it just my fantasy?*

I think it's your fantasy; I think it was more the experience of watching Freddy Laker and admiring him that drew me into the airline business.

But maybe subliminally, it could have been that my mother's experience and her stories of flying to South America might have had something to do with it.

I think the important thing is that I have never been interested in making money; I have never gone into a business to make money. That applies to every single business that I have started. I never thought of myself as a businessman. My very first venture I saw myself as an editor, not a businessman. I only became a businessman to make sure that I could stay an editor and to make sure that my magazine could survive. Therefore, the motivation of making money has never come into anything I've done. It has always been the challenge and the fact that I feel that I can enjoy it and do something better than has been done by other people. Overriding all this is that you only live once. And if you are in a position to do what you want to do, you might as well enjoy it.

Let me ask you a rather traditional question. If you were hit by a bus, what would happen to the company?

Well, in most of our companies, we have good managing directors running them. Basically, they have very little to do with me anyway. Their particular Virgin companies can just run on without me. Perhaps they might not expand quite as quickly as they would have done if I was around. And that might be a good thing in any event. So, I don't think my demise would be that damaging to Virgin in its present form. I am not a great believer in empires. Empires never survive, in any event. Therefore, I suspect the best thing the executors of the estate could do would be to try to arrange a lot of management buyouts of the various parts. To get lots of little, small Virgins around the world, which could hopefully build up into bigger Virgins. Then, when the new owners get hit by a bus, the same thing could happen again.

When you leave Virgin, what kind of enduring mark do you want to leave behind? How do you want to be remembered?

I think that it would be nice if Virgin can be remembered as a company that challenged the established way of doing things and built up a number of companies that were world leaders in their own field. That doesn't necessarily mean being the biggest companies, but the best in that particular field. I also would like that the staff of Virgin would have very happy memories of their time that they spent working here.

I sometimes wake up at night and lie there and think, "Is it all a dream?" Because it has been pretty good to date. It just seems almost too much for one man in one lifetime. So, if I am to reflect, I have been very fortunate to have so many wonderful experiences. Every day is fascinating. Every day, I am learning something new.

KEY POINTS

Virgin's Unique Competitive Edge:

The creative talents of individual employees

- Corporate culture.
  - Putting the world "right."
  - The notion of "family"; "People are our greatest asset."
  - Cultural glue based on sense of community, bonds of group, not codified.
  - Friendly, egalitarian, nonhierarchical atmosphere.
  - Anybody with a crazy idea gets a hearing.
  - Empowerment: "We're in the business of making millionaires."
  - Motivating people is key to organization's success: "If your staff is enjoying their work, they will perform well. Consequently, customers will enjoy their experience with your company."
  - Staff should have happy memories of their time in the organization.
- Leadership style
  - Reassuring contact with followers.
  - Social worker, both with followers and in vision for new products (e.g., Mates condoms).
  - Pragmatic idealist.
  - Extremely competitive.
  - Counterbalanced by strong executive role constellation.
  - Top person should enjoy himself so that others will feel free to have fun.
  - "Renaissance entrepreneur": 100 percent involvement in startup of new ventures, then delegate.
- Organizational design
  - Truly entrepreneurial and intrapreneurial organization.
  - Organic growth rather than acquisition.
  - "Small is beautiful"; small, autonomous units, small head office.
  - Work as an exciting adventure, challenging the status quo.
  - "If you do something for fun and create the best possible product, then the profit will come."

  – No formal board meetings; employees encouraged to contact Branson directly with ideas, problems.
  – "Communication from bottom to top"; lateral communication.
  – Speed: employees get a quick response directly from Branson, or just "go ahead and do it."
- Continuous transformation and change
  – Share the wealth with people who have new ideas; create a sense of ownership.
  – Attract and develop mavericks.
  – Environment offers high degree of freedom and encourages original ideas.
  – Drive for change.
  – "Creative adaptation": avoiding the not-invented-here syndrome.
- Building a global organization
  – *Keiretsu*-like system: more than five hundred small companies around the world operating quasi-independently.

PART TWO

Percy Barnevik

CHAPTER FOUR

Percy Barnevik
The Integrator

In 1987, in record time, Percy Barnevik combined ASEA, a Swedish engineering group, with Brown Boveri, a Swiss competitor. Soon after, the managing director of the power plant division at Mitsubishi of Japan declared that "our greatest rival is no longer the U.S. firm General Electric. The one we have to be most on guard against is ABB."[1] A senior GE executive said: "The lights are going out all over Europe, and the buccaneers have been turned loose. Among them is Percy Barnevik—this Swede with a beard who swings from country to country like the actor Errol Flynn, cutting deals and forming alliances. . . . A convalescing GE power systems may find him the most formidable adversary it has ever faced."[2]

Despite ABB's worldwide presence, some critics still wonder whether the sum really is larger than the parts, or whether it would not be more valuable to break up the organization. The complexity of the company's matrix structure draws criticism from its own employees as well as outsiders; many feel that they no longer understand how the company functions. Is the "multidomestic" federalist design really the best way to structure the organization? In a conglomerate of this size, how can an executive committee be certain that messages filter accurately to the lower layers of the organization? And how can they know how well the messages are received? Do the professed synergies among frontline companies really take place? After all, lateral communication is more easily described than implemented. Some critics are concerned about the process of managing change. Has ABB been able to institutionalize the process of change? Finally, and most important, the complexity of the organization is mind-boggling; what are the implications of running a company that does not really have a national identity? What leadership skills are required to run such a "cultural salad" of companies? What lessons can be learned about leadership development and motivation from Percy Barnevik's career history?

Barnevik's leadership style provides intriguing material for an examination of the influence an individual personality has on an organization. In the early stages of his career, he did not hesitate to move into a new position where he knew he could perform. Ever since his appointment as CEO at Sandvik in 1975, Barnevik's *modus operandi* has been continuous transformation and change: trimming, focusing, and moving companies to keep them at peak performance levels in highly competitive markets. He is also one of the world's best-known executives. He instilled a global mind-set at all levels of his organization. His personal career trajectory as well as his leadership of various companies over the past twenty years have had a similar theme: do it again, only bigger.

At the end of 1996, Barnevik stepped down as CEO of ABB, ending his tenure as dramatically as the surprise merger announcement brought the company into being less than ten years previously. Stepping down also incidentally pulled the rug from under the feet of business observers by answering their perennial question of what he would do next. Speculation about the future of the company, particularly heated given the close identification of the company with its CEO, immediately intensified, only to fall off in a sense of anticlimax. ABB would clearly continue along organizational rails just as smooth as those on which its world-class locomotives run.

But what of the chief executive? What challenge would he rise to after being hailed for nearly a decade as the savior of Europe's heavy-engineering industry and the inspirational pioneer of a unique organizational design? The answer came in the spring of 1997, when he was asked to become chairman of Investor, the Wallenberg family's huge holding company, which owns large chunks of some of the world's best-known brands: the drug company Astra, Ericsson (telecommunications), Electrolux (household appliances), and the auto maker Saab. Investor has a phenomenally rich portfolio, but one that performs erratically. Reluctant to be drawn out too soon about the strategy for his new job, Barnevik never-theless confided that "there will be a certain degree of impatience, a certain degree of raising demands, a certain degree of bench-marking."[3] He did not rule out divestment or possible future merg-ers. Even these brief comments rang a familiar note in the ears of Barnevik-watchers. Will Investor now draw the same media atten-tion in the first decade of the twenty-first century that ABB has had throughout the 1990s? In ten years' time, when even Barnevik will be thinking about his retirement, are commentators still going to be asking excitedly what he will do next?

The case study that follows in Chapter Five, "Percy Barnevik and ABB," traces his early cultural, developmental, and career his-tory and his tenure as CEO of ABB, and it closely examines the person-organization interface. It illustrates how his personal back-ground strongly influenced his way of designing and managing this sprawling engineering group.

The case explores the kind of leadership practices necessary to run a corporation effectively into the next century. Given his unique talent as an organizational architect, Barnevik is an ideal point of focus in the study of both organization and leadership. The personal background provided in the case allows exploration of a number of the psychodynamic issues affecting leadership. The interview, when he was CEO of ABB, adds significantly to the busi-ness world's understanding of Barnevik's leadership style.

ABOUT THE CASE

ABB is a truly transnational company. It has 210,000 employees in 140 countries, working in twelve hundred companies divided into five thousand profit centers. The case begins by describing how Barnevik set up this large, complex organization and subsequently managed it.

Barnevik's determination to turn ABB into one of the world's premier companies has given him enormous visibility. In press reports, he seems larger than life. His energy, drive, and ability to process massive amounts of information are legendary. It is clear that his personal and cultural background determined his personal *Weltanschauung,* which in turn colored the way he designed his organization. It could be said that he has organized ABB into five thousand "printing shops," because he learned early on in his parents' print shop the relationships between size, motivation, and customer responsiveness.

As a Swede, Barnevik's cultural background has also proved advantageous. The basic assumption of most Swedes is that "man is good." Stemming from their nonauthoritarian child-rearing style, this trustful attitude toward life limits paranoid dispositions and makes people more considerate and caring. Swedish national character reflects openness, honesty, reliability, directness, practicality, unpretentiousness, independence, and self-reliance. Swedes tend to be good at teamwork, conflict resolution, and information sharing. They are generally prepared and ready to work abroad. They believe in "workfare" (nobody should be idle), designing the job to fit the person and not the other way around, maintaining a long-term business orientation, and integrating social concerns with work. As a result, for a relatively small country Sweden has produced a remarkable number of world-class business leaders and companies. In addition, Swedes are generally not intimidated by authority. On the contrary, they are willing to challenge authority when they believe it to be wrong. Swedish culture also strongly values delegation and decentralization, patterns that very much fit the design of the modern organization. All of these characteristics help empower executives and limit potential leadership pathology.

It is worth repeating that Swedes tend to have a long-term view of things. They like to make contributions that benefit society at large, that transcend narrow business concerns. In their business practices, they go beyond ritualistic dedication to increasing shareholders' wealth. This attitude is reflected in Barnevik's vision for ABB. An emphasis on producing energy with minimal environmental impact is one result of this philosophy. ABB's investments in Eastern Europe and Asia also reflect implementation of this policy, which transcends the more traditional goal of profit maximization. As a caveat, it appears from his statements that Barnevik seems slightly apologetic about having this kind of business orientation, perhaps because he does not wish to seem "boastful or bombastic," as he puts it, about ABB's accomplishments in this area.

Closely related to the discussion of Barnevik's personal and cultural heritage is the question of leadership style and its link with personality. The case illustrates many aspects of his style that combine to make him an extremely effective leader. He has many telling beliefs about decentralization, speed, action orientation, directness, and equality. His leadership style minimizes the level of politicization in ABB. With Percy Barnevik, what you see is usually what you get.

As you read, think about what it means to be the head of a large organization as complex as ABB. How should a CEO set priorities? You should also consider the kind of pressure one is exposed to in such a position. CEOs, particularly of influential organizations, can very quickly become addicted to the power they wield; dysfunctional consequences are entirely possible. The CEO who finds himself in a hall of mirrors, surrounded by yes-men, hearing what he wants to hear brings distrust into the corporate culture—with potentially fatal ramifications. Although to some degree this is inevitable in that subordinates, awed by authority figures, often say what they think the boss wants to hear, Barnevik makes a valiant attempt to minimize the effects.

Barnevik excels in the charismatic and architectural dimensions of leadership. He laid out a clear road map for his employees at ABB. He knows how to develop a vision, articulate it, share it, and enact it. He spends an extraordinary amount of time energizing his employees, as his travel schedule and phone bills attest. He is an expert at networking, regularly contacting hundreds of people. The result of his leadership style is one of the most innovative large organizations in the world.

Barnevik demonstrates an interesting combination of micro and macro management. He is not reluctant to bypass; he is prepared to enter any level in the organization—a pattern of behavior that can be very disturbing to some of his subordinates. At times, he devotes his attention to detail, but he always retains the big picture. He has a "helicopter view" when dealing with cognitive complexity and processing large amounts of information. He strongly believes that the members of the *Konzernleitung* (executive committee), himself included, should be team players, which is not an easy task given that five nationalities are represented in the group. He also stresses the role of generativity in the organization, questioning whether an executive is a "giver" or a "receiver." He realizes that if his executives do not develop their people, do not act as mentors to the next generation, then ABB is not a learning organization and the company will eventually self-destruct. He also possesses a sense of cultural relativity and accepts and uses the strong points of different cultures, acknowledging that there are many equally valid ways of doing things. Of course, such an attitude is the *sine qua non* in a genuinely transnational company such as ABB.

Barnevik also seems to be endowed with remarkable drive and energy. If there is such a thing as the hardy personality, he certainly fits the description. It should be noted that *hardiness* is a concept taken from psychosomatic medicine, indicating a type of person who is more resistant to stress. Characteristics of hardiness are internal locus of control, positive involvement in the job, and openness to change—descriptions that certainly fit Percy Barnevik, as we shall see.

CHAPTER FIVE

Percy Barnevik and ABB

THE EARLY YEARS[1]

Percy Barnevik was born into a relatively well-to-do family on February 13, 1941, in Simrishamn, a small town in the south of Sweden on the Baltic sea. He is the last of his parents' three children and has a brother and a sister. Soon after his birth, the family moved to Uddevalla, where his father initially worked for the local newspaper before starting his own printing business. Percy spent most of his childhood years on the barren, windswept western coast of Sweden, where a strict Lutheran work ethic was impressed on him daily by his environment and his parents. Waste, inefficiency, indecisiveness, and disorderly conduct were frowned upon: you earned your bread by the sweat of your brow. His mother, sister, and brother helped out in the family business, and the youthful Barnevik himself worked as a typesetter in his spare time. He, his parents, and the employees would often put in long hours and work weekends to get a job done on time. These early years may have taught him that there was no such thing as a free lunch; you could only achieve something through hard work. His work in the little print shop gave him tools for survival and success that he has used throughout his life. He learned the value of commitment, of deadlines and speed, and above all of service to the customer. It also taught him about stress and how to cope with it.

This way of working was what drove him through his school career. Percy was determined to be the best student in the class. He was the pupil who always had an answer ready when the teacher asked a question. Even then, he was intolerant about wasting time. Unlike many of his contemporaries, he liked to familiarize himself with the syllabus well in advance and typically covered the school year's work long before the classes had even started. To this day, it is known that he hates doing anything without preparing for it well in advance and is always ready with all the information he needs whenever it is required. At school, he became impatient when discussion turned into digression or the class went too slowly for him. It was not that he was arrogant or felt superior to those less gifted than himself; rather, he probably felt that time was being wasted, time that could be more productively used elsewhere. He is well aware that this kind of behavior has continued into the present. Eberhard von Koerber, who was one of his colleagues on ABB's *Konzernleitung* or executive committee, calls this behavior pattern "constructive impatience." Barnevik realizes that not everyone can react as quickly or be as well prepared as he is, and that this makes him a demanding boss. Despite his attempts to control his impatience, he is often told by some of his long-term collaborators that he is still as impatient as ever.

He has always been competitive. When younger, he participated in national yachting competitions with his older brother Willy and won quite a few races. At the Gothenburg School of Economics, he constantly set himself and his closest friend at the time, Seth-Roland Arnér, greater standards of academic achievement. Even now, he hates not winning when he plays tennis with his old-time associate, Arne Bennborn, one of the senior VPs. Bennborn has even accused him of changing the rules when he is losing.

After he completed secondary school, like all young men in Sweden Barnevik was required to complete fifteen months of military service. He had already known before he joined the military that he possessed above-average staying power, but the military really proved it to him. He was the only one among the recruits who never grumbled and continued doggedly on his way until his objectives were achieved. He was made platoon commander.

Barnevik never considered himself to be a social person. He did go to school dances but was not a good dancer. He never smoked and seldom drank. People considered him too serious and distant. He always seemed to be preoccupied and in a hurry. They acknowledged, however, that once they knew him better, they would discover his dry sense of humor.

He never tried to impress the girls at secondary school, who were the majority in class. Unlike many young men, he did not spend a lot of time on relationships with women. He met Aina, his wife, when they were both at secondary school; they got married after she completed her studies, while he was still a student.

He was only nineteen when he was admitted to the Gothenburg School of Economics. While there, he pursued his studies with the same vigor, purposefulness, perfectionism, and dedication with which he had done everything so far. He honed his analytic and evaluative skills; if some of his classmates at the time can be believed, he did this by assessing new ideas of others' rather than by coming up with them himself. Ulf Saardahl, one of his classmates, says that there were two camps at school: those who were happy just to pass exams, and those for whom grades were very important. Barnevik tended to argue that he should be regraded whenever he was not the best student in each course. Saardahl said that this single-mindedness gave his classmates the impression that Barnevik must have had a boring time at Gothenburg.

During his studies, he seemed not to give much thought to the kind of career he would like to have when he left. He was interested in research, however, so he decided to enroll for a licentiate in philosophy, a degree that would link him more deeply with academia.

As part of his licentiate program, he was required to do an internship, which he completed with Mölnlycke, a major producer of pulp and paper in Sweden. Here, he had a great piece of luck. The models he created during his internship impressed a group of consultants from the Stanford Research Institute to such a degree that they arranged for Barnevik to receive a scholarship at Stanford University (1965–66), where he specialized in business administration and computer science and took the opportunity to travel all over the United States. His stay at Stanford convinced him that he did not want an academic career. When he returned home, to the great disappointment of his professors he discontinued his licentiate studies at Gothenburg. With hindsight, he saw this as the first major turning point in his life.

THE APPRENTICESHIP YEARS

When he returned from California in 1966, Barnevik decided to join the newly formed consulting company Datema. At the time, this was a real opportunity. Datema was run by an entrepreneur with an enlightened management philosophy who encouraged his employees to make their own decisions and to take responsibility. The company was experiencing explosive growth, and the young consultants were very much on their own since there was really no one to turn to for advice. The time Barnevik spent at Datema was a true learning experience. With his usual willingness to volunteer for things, he was given more and more responsibility and was finally asked to manage systems development for the conglomerate Axel Johnson Group. There he had to work with shipyards, construction companies, a steel company, an oil company, and a shipping company, among others. This meant, in effect, that he was considered a member of Datema's senior management team and was given responsibilities commensurate with that role.

Datema's president appreciated Barnevik's seriousness, openness to others, and his ability to assimilate data. Barnevik made frequent visits to the library, where he accumulated a vast store of knowledge that supported him in arguments with colleagues and clients and allowed him to work at a pace that few could match. To this day, rapidity and long working days have characterized his performance in every job he has done.

He had a habit of double-booking, or even triple-booking, his agenda so that he could pick the appointments that seemed most interesting. Sometimes he would give his colleagues appointments at strange times and for odd durations (at 12:07 for eight minutes, for example), but in fact he always had more time at his disposal if the matter under discussion interested him.

After about three years with Datema, Barnevik was consulted by Sandvik, a major Swedish specialty steel and tool company, which was having trouble with developing their information systems. It was clear to Barnevik what steps had to be taken to solve the problem. In a matter of days after his initial meeting with Sandvik, he produced a report with major recommendations. As a result, the company made him an offer (far in excess of what he was earning at Datema) to implement his recommendations.

Barnevik accepted their offer only when they gave him the freedom to select the people who would work for him. He was not about to go into his first real-life situation with his hands tied and his operational space confined in any way. He joined Sandvik on December 1, 1969.

LEARNING FROM EXPERIENCE

Barnevik hired around one hundred fifty people in 1969 and 1970. He had contacted some of these people before he officially joined Sandvik, using the extensive network he had cultivated while at Datema and his ability to convince people to buy into his ideas to attract a highly qualified group of people. One of the people hired by Barnevik at the time recalls: "It was impossible to stand up to Percy. He called me and said that he wanted to see me the next day for an interview. I told him it was not possible because I was going to fly to Australia. He told me that I would have to change the reservation because the interview was already scheduled and he had even checked which train I could take. I went to the interview, got the job, and have never had any reason to regret it."[2]

Barnevik hired people he could rely on, people to whom he could delegate, and people whom he could trust. Some of them—like Bengt Skantze (now head of corporate development at ABB), whom he had known from Datema—are still working for him. Because of his long association with close collaborators, communication tended to require few words. He could always rely on them to execute whatever suggestion he made.

As the head of administrative development, he was hired to develop the company's new information systems and to rationalize its administrative functions. Typically, he expanded the role and gave himself additional responsibility. The original job of administrative development and information systems soon went to the back burner as he spent more time troubleshooting and restructuring Sandvik companies in Asia, Africa, Europe, South America, and North America. As might be expected, he accomplished most of the tasks successfully. He would approach a problem, suggest multiple solutions to it, and put all of these into a comprehensive, well-reasoned report that he would then present to the board and use as an argument to convince them that the changes he was proposing were really necessary. For a company hitherto very traditionally managed, Barnevik was like a whirlwind. He acted less from desire to make a name or career for himself than from conviction that there were many things wrong with the company and he had to make it more effective. Carl-Eric Björkegren, his superior at the time, said of him, "Barnevik was extremely intelligent and ambitious. The only thing I had to teach him was to laugh, but he loosened up as time went on."

Barnevik's drive and energy were rewarded in 1973 when he was offered an additional job as group controller at Sandvik, while keeping his earlier position. This meant that what he had been doing all along was now sanctioned through an official position. In addition, the responsibility for financial matters was added to his administrative portfolio.

BECOMING A TOP EXECUTIVE

In 1975, Barnevik accepted appointment as CEO of the U.S. subsidiary Sandvik Steel, whose performance at the time was rather weak. Sandvik had so far not been able to really penetrate the big U.S. market. He approached the assignment, as he approached any new challenge, with dedication and a will to make a difference, to turn the company around quickly. He managed to rationalize operations to triple sales to $250 million and make the company profitable in the four years he was there. With hindsight, however, it can be seen that he made some strategic errors. But then again, he would never have learned that they were errors had he not made them. This confirmed his opinion that it is better to act than to do nothing; there is something to be said for learning from one's mistakes. As he once stated in an interview: "You have to accept a fair share of mistakes. I tell my people that if we make 100 decisions and 70 turn out to be right, that's good enough. I'd rather be roughly right than slow. . . . Why emphasize speed at the expense of precision? Because the costs of delay are vastly greater than the occasional mistake."[3]

His second stay in the United States, this time as a businessman, taught him the importance of having the freedom to be able to operate in a large, open market unconstrained by artificial boundaries. He has often thought back to his experience of building the Sandvik business in the United States, and in particular the direct interface with the many customer groups there. He enjoyed acting in the field; it was a major achievement to take the market share in cutting tools from such formidable domestic competitors as U.S. Steel and GE. He returned to Sweden to take up the position of executive vice president of finance and administration for Sandvik, with the opportunity of becoming CEO within a few years, but he did not stay long in that job. A year after his return, he was invited to become CEO of ASEA.

ASEA'S TRANSFORMATION WIZARD

In 1979, the Swedish company ASEA was slow-growing but respected, one of the ten largest electrical engineering companies in the world and technically a world-class company with some forty thousand employees, three-fourths of them in Sweden. Economically and financially, however, ASEA was in bad shape. There was excess capacity in its markets, demand was weakening, and profits were falling steadily. In addition to these external factors, the company had a centralized, bureaucratic internal structure as well as serious morale problems.

ASEA had a long tradition and history as an engineering company. It afforded its employees secure employment, took care of them in a patriarchal way, and selected and promoted managers on the basis of their technical competence rather than business acumen. No personnel had been discharged since the 1930s—a policy assiduously maintained even through the difficult years of the late 1970s. ASEA did however, have leading-edge products in a number of areas that were growing and profitable.

This was just the type of invitation Barnevik relished. The challenge was to impose himself, as a nonengineer, on an engineering-dominated company, change the attitudes of complacency and apathy that prevailed among the work force, and turn it around as quickly as possible. He felt that he had to move fast, because he needed to reposition the company and nurse it back to health so as to benefit from the anticipated market upturn in the heavy electrical-goods industry in the last years of the century. He imposed only one condition: he needed the board of directors' full support for the radical surgery he believed was necessary. Since he had been selected by Curt Nicolin, then chairman of the board, and by Marcus Wallenberg, the dominant shareholder and honorary chairman, the rest of the board (who were all engineers) could do nothing but grudgingly approve. Some of them thought, however, that the job would be too much for him and that he would have to leave without completing his assignment.

As usual, Barnevik prepared himself intensively before assuming his responsibilities. Long before he left Sandvik, he read everything available about ASEA and got some ASEA engineers to teach him about their business. One of his colleagues recalls: "I met him at a recreation area accompanying his two sons, who were skiing. He had his dog's leash in one hand, and at the same time he was deeply absorbed in a physics book that he held in his other hand."[4]

When he took up his position, he handpicked a small group of ASEA executives, representing a variety of disciplines, to be his personal consultants and catalysts. "Percy's Boys" (who included one woman) were briefed to help him analyze the issues facing the company.

Barnevik knew, when he assumed his new position, that gradual change would have no effect in this company. ASEA needed a radical shake-up that would shock the company into action. Neither did he want the process to drag out and create too much uncertainty, preventing the company from refocusing quickly. Doing this was difficult, but he made two fundamental structural changes.

The first was to delayer the organization and reorganize it into a global matrix once the company had expanded internationally; the second was to get rid of the bureaucracy of the corporate head office. In doing this he used a simple rule of thumb: the 30 percent rule. He passionately believed that bureaucracy generates waste; for that reason, he broke it down by assuming that 30 percent of central staff could be spun off into separate and independent profit centers, another 30 percent could be transferred to the operational companies as part of their overhead, 30 percent could be eliminated as superfluous to requirements, and the remaining 10 percent could be kept on at headquarters as the minimum required. He was driven by the conviction that what was needed were business units that were self-contained and situated as close as possible to the end consumer. His radical surgery at head office, where he reduced the number of employees from two thousand to two hundred, illustrated this philosophy in action.

In Sweden, this period of downsizing and delayering became known as "Barnevik's Reign of Terror," a label that still rankles him. Others called it ASEA's cultural revolution. According to Barnevik, people did not seem to understand his anguish in making such tough decisions. He felt they failed to realize that only an efficient and lean company could survive in a very competitive world.

He was lucky in that the climate in ASEA was more open to change than before, because of the company's deteriorating economic situation. (Some external analysts even believed it was beyond rescue and would drift into losses.) There was great willingness to accept that the old way of doing things was no longer workable. Bennborn, one of the old ASEA hands, was very helpful in the change process as he himself had previously tried, unsuccessfully, to get a number of similar changes accepted by the board. It was he who introduced Barnevik to the idea of being a multidomestic company (having deep roots in many different countries, having a local identity, respecting national differences and cultures), of being an insider rather than an invader. Bennborn also shared his views about matrix structures.

While he was engaged in the transformation process, Barnevik made a strong effort to communicate as much of what he was doing to as many people as possible, to avoid the spread of rumors and uncertainty. This included talking to union leaders and politicians and explaining what he wanted to accomplish—a very different approach from the previous regime, which had regarded those constituencies as a threat. Eventually, his radical changes yielded returns. During the seven years he spent as CEO at ASEA, the company's turnover quadrupled, earnings rose eightfold, and market capitalization multiplied twenty times.

Barnevik did not stop there. Looking at market trends, he believed strongly that there would be a shake-out in the electrical engineering industry and that ASEA had to become more international. Only those companies with a certain critical mass would be able to survive and benefit from the upturn he predicted. He knew that ASEA needed to expand radically and internationally, and that the only way to do so was by acquiring companies wherever he could find them. After the first two or three years, ASEA was in better shape, and he started to build presence in the neighboring countries to make all of Scandinavia a home market.

Important major acquisitions were Strömberg in Finland in 1986, and Elektrisk Bureau in Norway in 1987. A few years earlier, he had tried to acquire a major part of the ailing German giant AEG, which was teetering on the brink of disaster, but the Germans did not let him in. It was clear that he had to penetrate continental Europe as well, since Scandinavia would be too small as a home base for the upcoming battle. He also had his eye on the United States and tried to buy businesses from one of his major competitors, General Electric. He was thwarted, however, by the price that Jack Welch demanded. That was the point at which he decided to approach Brown, Boveri, and Co. in Switzerland, subsequently concluding the biggest cross-border deal in Europe to date.

Barnevik's decision to talk to BBC was based on the pure logic of the fit between the two companies. ASEA operated in geographic areas and in some product spheres that on the whole complemented rather than competed with those of Brown Boveri. In such areas as power transmission, there was a major overlap, but if properly restructured the joint company would have a clear lead in size and competitiveness. A merger would add value to both companies. Both companies were traditional mainstays of their local environment that, if they remained isolated, would sooner or later have to allow themselves to be bought out or shut down. In addition, similarities between the Swiss and the Swedes suggested there would not be major temperamental fireworks: both groups of executives came from small nations and had sufficient international exposure to know they were dependent on the rest of the world for the survival of their companies. This would help avoid any kind of ethnocentrism in their behavior. (The biggest BBC national presence, Germany, was another story. The Germans didn't like being dominated by the Swiss or the Swedes.) Most important, though, the timing was right. Bennborn described it as window of opportunity, the kind that would only open once. It couldn't have been done ten years earlier or ten years later. An important factor was that although Brown Boveri had been four times the size of ASEA in 1980, by 1987 they were equals. A fifty-fifty merger required equality. In fact, since in 1987 ASEA was the more profitable of the two, it became difficult to conceive a fifty-fifty venture for that reason.

The two companies together represented a major global force to be reckoned with. The biggest hitch Barnevik saw in the deal was that both companies had to be integrated quickly, without adding too much bureaucracy and uncertainty. He was very much aware that the longer the courtship between the two companies, the more he would face criticism of a political nature. The whole merger could become quite messy if factors such as national pride (as in "we're giving away the crown jewels of our country"), debates about losing core technologies, and potential unemployment through restructuring were raised not just by employees and managers but also by politicians, union leaders, and the press. He had to prove his critics wrong. He had to show the major stakeholders that this type of organization would pay off—and for that, secrecy and speed were essential.

When the merger was announced on August 10, 1987, at simultaneous news conferences in Stockholm and Baden, Switzerland, it came as a total surprise. Business analysts had expected that something was going to happen, because Barnevik had been on the lookout for suitable acquisitions for quite some time. But he managed to sidestep them all by the sheer magnitude of the undertaking. Confidentiality was maintained by the inner circles of the two companies during the negotiations; he insisted on secrecy all along, and nobody outside knew anything about the merger. Rapid closure of the deal was facilitated by the fact that he had the support of the dominant shareholders of the two companies, Stephan Schmidheiny (Brown Boveri) and the Wallenberg family (ASEA). Given that they supported the spirit and rationale behind the merger, it was just a matter of time before it was finalized. Barnevik managed to complete the whole process in six weeks. He dispensed with all but the most basic aspects of due-diligence exercises—a highly risky move in any circumstances, but he felt the risk to be minimal and the potential returns disproportionately large.

INTEGRATING ASEA AND BROWN BOVERI

Speed was a very important factor both before and after the merger. Barnevik wanted to get the integration process over and done with as quickly as possible, because he felt it was better to avoid confusion and loss of market share[5] and he believed that it was "better to move swiftly and correct an error here and there afterwards, rather than leave people hanging in the air, uncertain about their future."[6]

He moved extraordinarily swiftly. Arne Olsson, head of management resources at ABB, remembers: "I thought that he was really running at top speed before the merger, that there were no more gears left. I thought he was in overdrive. But, damn it, when the merger was taking place he moved up another gear. He accelerated. . . ."[7]

As he had done when he joined ASEA, Barnevik now set out to identify those key executives who would play the role of trusted lieutenants to make the new corporation work. He decided that these global executives had to be "people capable of becoming superstars—tough-skinned individuals, who were fast on their feet, had good technical and commercial backgrounds, and had demonstrated the ability to lead others."[8]

Their most important characteristics would include "patience, good language ability, stamina, work experience in at least two or three countries, and, most important, humility and respect for other cultures."[9]

> Global managers have exceptionally open minds. They respect how different countries do things, and they have the imagination to appreciate why they do them that way. But they are also incisive; they push the limits of the culture. Global managers don't passively accept it when someone says, "You can't do that in Italy or Spain because of the unions," or "You can't do that in Japan because of the Ministry of Finance." They sort through the debris of cultural excuses and find opportunities to innovate. . . . Global managers are also generous and patient. They can handle the frustrations of language barriers.[10]

In Barnevik's own words: "But beyond all these characteristics they need another quality: do they develop their people? Is the person a 'giver' or a 'receiver'? The giver makes people available to other parts of the organization; the receiver needs people all the time."[11]

At the same time, he considered having thousands of global managers unnecessary. He believed that to work well ABB needed five hundred or so global managers, people who were internationally minded but also comfortable with their nation of origin.

During this period he and his top management team, as well as people from the human resource departments of both companies, were interviewing virtually around the clock to identify the individuals who were best suited to become global managers. Barnevik estimated that he personally conducted some five hundred interviews and could not recall another period in his life when he worked so intensively.

Then, in 1988, after completing the interviews and identifying his superstars, came Cannes.

Barnevik felt that he needed to share his vision of the company with his people and give them a framework within which to do business. Just five months after the merger, he invited 250 of them to Cannes for a three-day seminar during which he laid out his way of looking at ABB, as the new company was to be called. He went through a staggering 198 slides—a chore even by his standards—and impressed his people immensely, explaining the principles upon which the merged company would operate, introducing a twenty-one page corporate policy bible, and requesting his audience to transmit all of what he had told them to the next layer of management (thirty thousand of them worldwide) within the following sixty days. He always believed that open communication was the key to successful business.

Barnevik's next task was to streamline ABB. Just as he had done at ASEA, he set out to reduce the size of corporate headquarters, using the same 30 percent rule, and began decentralizing the operations of most of the subsidiaries into independent profit centers. He implemented a radical redeployment of human, technological, and financial resources by making them the responsibility of the frontline companies. For example, instead of having centralized corporate laboratories for developing technology, centers of excellence were created that were closely linked to operating companies excelling in specific technological developments. The outcome of technological innovation was then leveraged throughout the organization. Only 150 people remained at the head office. Not surprisingly, this policy met resistance from the workforce and from those who were to lose their jobs. These were tough days, even for Barnevik. It is never easy to tell people that they are redundant, and even less so if in other circumstances these people would be among the organization's best assets. In the end, the company came through the process better, leaner, and readier to compete in world markets.

A great deal of work had to be done, though, to make this cross-border merger work. Probably the most far-reaching change Barnevik implemented in the new company was to introduce the global matrix he used at ASEA. ABB now had a cadre of 250 "global" executives located in almost 150 countries. Göran Lindahl (a member of the *Konzernleitung*) calls this type of organizational architecture "decentralization under central conditions."[12] In a sense, it turns ABB into a federation of companies. Barnevik himself, and twelve executive vice presidents (the number was later reduced to seven), formed the company's supreme decision-making body (the *Konzernleitung*). On a macro level, they negotiated broad targets (defined in terms of growth, profit, and return on capital employed) for each business and geographic area. In addition, they created the top management forum, which consists of some four hundred managers from country and operational regions. Since 1993, the forum has also included a top management council, made up of seventy senior managers who meet three times a year.

To control this gigantic operation, Barnevik required from each profit center dollar-based monthly profit-and-loss and balance sheets, to be delivered to the head office on the tenth of each month. To reduce time spent in decision making, each region had its own control headquarters; the most important matters, however, were referred to Zürich. Every three weeks, a Konzernleitung meeting would devote an entire day to strategic and operational issues.

The matrix can be viewed as a spreadsheet. On the spreadsheet the column headings were the "business segments," further subdivided into business areas (BAs). At the top of each segment sat a *Konzernleitung* member, who reported on the performance of that segment as if it were a separate entity (for example, the member responsible for the power-generation segment reported on the worldwide performance of that segment). Similarly, each individual business area regarded itself as a worldwide business and reported in that manner. The horizontal axis listed the various companies by country. ABB's world was divided up into regions (the Americas, Asia, Europe) or groupings of countries at the head of which sat a *Konzernleitung* member. A company within a country—a motor company, for example—would report both to a global manager for motors and to the country manager.

The important thing was that the global business-area manager and the country manager should understand their complementary and differing roles. The BA manager set the framework: who would develop and produce what, what export markets would be allocated to each company, and so on. The BA manager also watched the global quality and standards and safeguarded cross-border transfer of technologies and best practices. The country manager supervised the day-to-day business and was supportive in domestic market networking, recruitment, union matters, and the like. Sometimes the two managers would have different opinions, for example, if the country company ran into trouble. It was important, therefore, to train people in how to manage the conflict inherent in this situation.

To limit the possibility of conflict, all major issues had to be discussed by the BA manager and the country manager. Disagreements were referred to the *Konzernleitung* member to whom the BA manager and country manager reported. In the rare event of irreconcilable conflict, the matter would be passed up to the *Konzernleitung* as a whole, and to the group CEO. The executive committee made it quite clear, however, that such situations should be the exception rather than the rule. Regular conflicts indicated that both BA manager and country manager should look for another job. Barnevik once said that if a problem was brought to him more than twice, the quarreling managers would both be fired—an exaggeration, but also an indication that there is a limit to patience.

In spite of the potential for conflict, Barnevik felt that his matrix was a relatively simple model, and he believed the inherent contradictions within the company could easily be resolved. In his model, top executives spell out broad policy guidelines and challenge the status quo; middle management integrates strategy horizontally, leverages technology, and transfers best practices; while frontline executives take on an entrepreneurial role. The CEO explained to William Taylor of the *Harvard Business Review*:

> ABB is an organization with three internal contradictions. We want to be global and local, big and small, and radically decentralized

with centralized reporting and control. If we resolve these contradictions, we create real organizational advantage. . . .

You want to be able to optimize a business globally—to specialize in the production of components, to drive economies of scale as far as you can, to rotate managers and technologists around the world to share expertise and solve problems. But you also want to have deep local roots everywhere you operate—building products in the countries where you sell them, recruiting the best local talent from the universities, working with the local government to increase exports. If you build such an organization, you create a business advantage that is damn difficult to copy. . . .

The matrix is the framework through which we organize our activities. It allows us to optimize our business globally *and* maximize performance in every country in which we operate. Some people resist it. They say the matrix is too rigid, too simplistic. But what choice do you have? To say you don't like a matrix is [to say] you don't like factories or you don't like breathing. It's a fact of life. If you deny the formal matrix, you wind up with an informal one—and that's much harder to reckon with. . . .[13]

There was a major flaw in the matrix structure Barnevik used. For the people who were "at an intersection," reporting to two bosses (each of whom might have differing objectives), the matrix could be traumatic. For some, it was never completely clear what the criteria were for success in the job nor which of the bosses had precedence over the other. Realizing that organizations can only be as good as the people working in them, ABB has addressed this problem by going out of its way to clarify roles and make the mechanism of resolving conflicts work.

Nobody knew better than Barnevik how much effort it took to maintain the matrix; there was always a tendency for some executives to suboptimize, to transgress the rules of the matrix, and to do something advantageous for their own unit at the expense of somebody else's. Bennborn once said they knew that a matrix structure to some extent goes against human nature, but they just had to push and push and make it work.

Nevertheless, Barnevik created an organization that was not only lean and flexible and decentralized enough to operate anywhere in the world (thanks to the ABACUS information system, which provided data to the frontline operations and helped group management evaluate performance) but could also benefit from the economies of scale of looking at the world as a single market. The dream he had when he was in the United States of operating in a single worldwide market was now almost reality.

RUNNING ABB

Top executives at ABB firmly believed that there would be an upturn in the electrical engineering market as the recession of the early 1990s in the industrialized world receded, but to capitalize upon it companies would have to be located throughout the world with the same market presence and the same commitment to the customer in every area. Because of the global nature of ABB, top executives felt they succeeded in spreading the risk and reducing the prospect of economic setbacks that may occur in any one country or region.

To be present in all areas of the world, Barnevik acquired companies wherever ABB was not strong. In total, he accumulated around 150 companies, the most important of which are Fläkt in Sweden, Strömberg in Finland, EB in Norway, Zamech in Poland, First Brno in the Czech Republic, the CCC companies in Spain, Westinghouse's power distribution and transmission units, British Rail Engineering in the UK, and Combustion Engineering in the United States—the last one being by far the largest acquisition the company has ever made. Through these acquisitions, he managed to establish ABB as a presence in each of the world's major markets. He has always adopted the same tactics he used in acquiring Strömberg or in the merger that created ABB; he could sometimes decide, negotiate, and buy long before his competitors even became aware of what was happening. He was particularly stimulated by his ventures in Eastern Europe, where ABB is currently one of the largest investors. Politicians talk a lot about getting Eastern Europe on its feet, but Barnevik felt that ABB could do something about it. (There are some twenty thousand people working for ABB in forty operating companies in the region.) This exposed him to criticism; it has been said that he did it more for ideological reasons than from sound business logic. Barnevik felt he need not excuse his actions to shareholders, since most acquired companies are turned around within two years and Eastern Europe as a whole is profitable now. Some of the companies acquired early on are now highly profitable.

Barnevik also turned to Asia, which he saw as a region with enormous potential for the products made by ABB. Asian acquisitions proved more difficult, but Barnevik tried to handle the problem by stepping up efforts to establish greenfield plants (building a business, product line, or facility from scratch, as opposed to brownfield efforts—working with what exists) in addition to establishing joint ventures. ABB currently has more than sixty companies in operation in the Asian Pacific area.

Once a company has been bought, it is integrated into the ABB network as quickly and efficiently as possible. This means that wherever feasible ABB obtains a majority stock position. As Barnevik told *Fortune* magazine, "If you are going to run a global group and you have to consider minority interests all the time, it doesn't work."[14]

One of the ways he kept his executives at peak performance was periodically to shift responsibilities around, so that nobody has enough time to become complacent and ineffective in his or her work. He never spared any level of hierarchy from this constant change, not even the *Konzernleitung*. In August 1993, the committee was rationalized in a move to strengthen ABB's competitiveness and help the company adjust to the increase in regional trading blocks. Membership of the new *Konzernleitung* was cut from twelve to eight, and the six operating divisions were reduced to four. Barnevik changed the responsibilities of each member on the *Konzernleitung* and added or withdrew names from the list of members. He believed that if people at all levels of the organization are kept on their toes, the organization as a whole is encouraged to be flexible.

Running ABB now centers on two dynamics: expansion, and maintaining the momentum of the existing company, which depends on a culture of permanent revolution. This produces quite specific problems. It is difficult to maintain a sense of excitement and standards of peak performance when people feel insecure, as they inevitably do in a company that is in a constant state of change and has little time for the process of integration and formation of a stable culture. To a certain extent, the problems of this second dynamic are resolved by the first: ABB's ventures into Poland and China, and its commitment to tackling environmental problems in the old Eastern Bloc, are a real source of pride and motivation for employees. Nevertheless, there are equally real difficulties encountered in working for ABB, and Barnevik's legendary emphasis on speed is responsible for many of them. Has his vision been properly assimilated? Has a sense of commitment been transmitted? Molding acquired companies into a cultural whole takes time—and Barnevik made no secret of his preference for speed over other factors in the process of acquisition.

Barnevik's response to these difficulties might be to stress his belief in the importance of communication. That was the motivation behind the Cannes conference, where he defined the five core values of the company and initiated the procedure intended to transmit them to all levels of management:

1. Meeting customer needs
2. Decentralizing
3. Taking action
4. Respecting an ethic
5. Cooperating

The ABB values are reinforced through intensive in-house programs of executive education, in which members of the *Konzernleitung* invest a great deal of time. The prime values are meeting customer needs and decentralization. The former emphasizes that the customer always come first, and that everyone in the company has a responsibility to satisfy the customer's wishes. Each employee has to meet customers, even if this is not an obvious part of an individual job description. The latter, decentralization, is seen as the only way to defeat bureaucracy. By this means, responsibility is passed down the line to junior people, to motivate them and provide for the most efficient use of resources at the level where they are required. It is vital that this process be combined with efficient communication and proper supervision.

Taking action is perhaps the most personally motivated of the five basic values: prepare thoroughly; do not get bogged down in detail; do not investigate things to death; and above all, *be fast*. This effectively rules out management by committee. Committees are extremely rare inside ABB. Barnevik defined the fourth core value, respecting an ethic, as being reliable and honest in both internal dealings and relations with customers. It might seem idealistic to expect everybody to operate according to a sense of honor and honesty, but in fact the principle works.

The fifth core value, cooperation, is the one most frequently cited whenever change is imposed on the organization. Barnevik maintained that it does not really matter where somebody operates so long as the individual's talent remains within the ABB group. Applying this value causes a tremendous amount of paper to be transferred between desks. There is a tendency for the principle to be taken too literally, with people scrupulously informing everybody about everything. The operation can be counterproductive; when drenched with information, people tend to stop reading. A massive investment in an electronic network for communication is one way of reducing the paper problem.

Barnevik hoped that the principle of communication established at Cannes would evolve into the glue to bind the company together. It still has to be tested: will the glue hold against the tensions necessarily accompanying expansion, change, constantly increasing performance targets, and the inherent contradictions in the company's operational structure? Some observers wonder whether a company consisting of numerous constituencies in different countries and with no common first language can be molded into a coherent whole. A fluid environment, in which people are constantly shifting around, can leave them cynical and unresponsive. Good figures are met with a demand for better; the *Konzernleitung* consistently raises targets in response to high performance. This is known within the company as "stretch vision"; in some instances it has contributed to fear and demoralization, which might appear to undermine its motivating power.

BARNEVIK AND THE FUTURE OF ABB

When these sorts of questions and criticisms are raised, it is inevitably to the company's leader that one turns for an answer. Barnevik was such a force within ABB that there was a feeling that if it could be done, he was the one to do it. An undeniable sense of awe accompanies accounts of him—perhaps a mix that is equal parts fear and admiration. This lends weight to the idea that he is himself the principal ingredient of the glue that holds his company together, an irony considering that such a large part of his management philosophy is based on the principles of decentralization and local decision making.

Reflections about Barnevik as a man on the rise tended to stress his overseriousness. Carl-Eric Björkegren at Sandvik had to teach him to laugh; others considered him boring and noticed that he only came to life when he was excited over figures and profits. It is true that he is not good at small talk and has few interests outside business. He does not enjoy large, anonymous gatherings, preferring to mix with people at smaller, more intimate get-togethers. His disinclination for superficial social contact is counterbalanced by his conviction that personal communication is one of the most effective ways of motivating people, and his determination to establish an atmosphere of openness, trust, and respect within ABB.

Sometimes the candid elements of his personality can also have a demoralizing effect on his subordinates. One of his colleagues at Sandvik has said: "When you reported to Percy after having accomplished a job which you felt satisfied with, you still had the feeling that he could have done it better. This is very trying in the long run. This tended to create a feeling of inferiority among his subordinates, a feeling of insufficiency. At the same time, one has to keep in mind that Percy very rarely criticized anyone. On the contrary, he always tried to motivate his personnel. His competence, however, sometimes made you feel inadequate."[15]

Criticism of Barnevik, as here, is rarely unmixed; if his exigency, impatience, and pace are wearing, they seem simultaneously to arouse admiration. As his long-term collaborator, Arne Bennborn, has commented,

> . . . there is his pace. It is relentless. To illustrate, if you travel with him, you get up at 6:30 and they pick you up in a car at 7:30. And then you have a full morning of meetings, and lunch, more meetings, then dinner, and customers. Then you go back to the hotel at 11:00 or 11:30 in the evening to get up the next morning at 6:30 A.M. But Percy gets up at 3:00 A.M. because that is when they open the switchboard to Europe. He calls people in Europe between 3:00 and 6:00 A.M. And he does that every day, for a week.[16]

Barnevik's reluctance to talk about his own leadership style has done little to counteract the almost mythical accounts of his extraordinary capacity for work; indeed, his perpetual globe-trotting—traveling for up to two hundred days a year—and his half-joking comments (such as "I'm normally in my office two days a week, Saturday and Sunday") can only reinforce them. He is at the head office only one week each month, when he works twelve-hour days, from eight to eight. He can get by on four hours sleep a night. He takes a four-week family holiday every summer, sailing half the time, during which he is in constant contact with the head office by fax or telephone. He also goes on a two-to-three-week trip with his family every Christmas and New Year.

Despite the perennial difficulties of controlling an organization of such size, Barnevik was always open to his colleagues' points of view and always ready to bypass normal hierarchical relationships and exploit the network of the ABB matrix to gather information from different sources. Olsson of ABB draws a vivid portrait of him:

> You see the guy in action, he is really like two welding torches that go right through you. . . . People feel his intensity, this radiation almost, coming out of the man. It makes him a very demanding superior in terms of getting things done. He has an extremely high capacity for work. He has this ability to deal with a multitude of things at the same time, and to square away large volumes of work. . . . And then there is this onion-peeling capacity, this ability to ruthlessly get to the core of the matter fast. When you take up a problem with him and discuss it, you'd better be well prepared, because you know that he will spot your weaknesses. He wants to know that the whole thing fits together. . . . There is this bluntness, this speaking in straightforward language. . . .
>
> Being the way he is, it takes a bit of guts to tell him, "Look, I have another opinion." But when you dare to do so, while he looks at you, his dark, piercing eyes just drilling through your brain . . . if what you have said is good, it may come back to you in a memo from him, put in a larger framework. Then you can feel a little bit happy that what you said wasn't overlooked.
>
> He is equipped with capacities and capabilities which are simply not normal. He has this absolutely fantastic analytical capacity, good judgment, attention to detail, and intuition. The capacity to

switch back and forth between the big picture and paying attention to details is really a gift. In addition, he has a true ability to match individuals to specific needs in the company. . . . And then there is this never-ceasing drive to move ahead. . . . What pushes him is a tremendous urge to build and develop something, to change things, to move things forward, to make ABB into the leading elec- trotechnical engineering company in the world. He has this urge to make it happen. . . .[17]

Barnevik is at the peak of his career. He has the satisfaction of knowing that he has severely shaken the complacency of rival com- panies, even though ABB shows current profit levels significantly below the best in the industry. When asked if the shareholders got enough returns in the years he ran ASEA and ABB, Barnevik answers that the value of ASEA stock has risen more than fortyfold since 1979, or 30.5 percent per year, which is almost three times the stock index. (ASEA and Brown Boveri are still listed separately on their national stock exchanges.)

Since Barnevik has taken a more removed position as chairman of Investor, what will happen to ABB now that he is no longer there to guide it directly? Strong management is vital to keep together the kind of company he has created. He considered his *Konzern- leitung* adequately equipped to do so, but will others? With so much attention focused on him, and so much depending on his personal presence, the question remains: what will the company be like with- out his being closely involved?

Chapter Six

An Interview with Percy Barnevik

It is hard to ignore Percy Barnevik. The first impression[1] is that of a likable person, a tall, slightly stooped, handsome man with heavy glasses, piercing eyes, and a beard. He has a certain professorial presence—a career he almost chose. But if he had become an academic, he certainly would not have hidden in an ivory tower. On the contrary, whatever he says is quite earthy and direct.

Barnevik presents ideas with a certain forcefulness. At the start of any interview, because of his intensity, it is difficult not to be a little self-conscious in his presence. After all, here is a person who is the subject of many myths. Numerous anecdotes have been told about his style of leadership. Paradoxically, in spite of his awareness of his reputation, Barnevik also seems quite shy. He is not a natural extrovert, but more a person who has taught himself to behave that way. There may be an element of truth in his nickname: "the Greta Garbo of the business world." The contradictions are remarkable, but these are refreshing characteristics in a man running such a gigantic enterprise.

After the initial awkwardness has passed, the listener very quickly feels involved. Because of his intensity, Barnevik is not a person to whom one can feel indifferent. He is articulate and persuasive. He responds candidly to any question. He obviously believes strongly in what he is doing. He is a man with a mission—and a man in a hurry. Barnevik is trying to revolutionize organizations and cannot wait. He is a prophet who wants to leave behind a different but better world, and he obviously believes ABB is the vehicle for doing so. Much has to be accomplished, and there is so little time in which to do it. As Barnevik begins presenting his ideas about the future of the company, he becomes very animated and blossoms. Unwittingly, the listener is caught up in his web of ideas and shares his enthusiasm.

What is also noticeable is Barnevik's humility, despite the enormous power he wields. Success has not gone to his head. He has no airs; he does not play games with his interlocutor. He certainly knows how to keep whatever narcissistic disposition he possesses under control. In discussion, he continuously downplays his own contribution to the success of ABB and gives much of the credit to others.

Barnevik is well aware of the influence he has over others and realizes that he can be intimidating. Although he is definitely action-oriented, he also possesses a certain reflective side. He has learned that to be successful at his job it is not enough just to be an efficient technocrat. Thus he makes a strong effort to put others at ease. He has even taught himself to engage in small talk; once he gets over his shyness, a wry sense of humor emerges.

An additional side to his personality, surprising in someone who has been called "Mr. Lean and Mean," is the sense of humanity that runs through the conversation. One hears a deep concern for the welfare of his people. He regularly mentions the need for empathy. It is clear that he goes through a lot of soul searching before he makes decisions that affect the lives of others. Restructuring has obviously taken a psychological toll.

Could you say something about the architecture of your global organization?

The fundamental organizational design that ABB is known for is its extreme decentralization. This obsession with decentralization has been a theme throughout my whole career. I have seen the deficiencies of the big corporation, the dangers of bureaucracy, the effects of the ivory tower, where people sit in their rooms, far away from their customers, the lack of engagement and absence of entrepreneurial spirit. I'm sure you've heard the story of the person coming into a big office who asks, "How many people are working here?" and gets the answer, "Half of them." This may be a worn-out old joke, but there is some truth behind it.

I remember coming to inspect ASEA for the first time in 1979 and seeing that huge glass-and-plastic building with four thousand engineers, each in their room. And I wondered whether they ever saw a customer. In the company I came from, Sandvik, we had a rule that no workshop should be bigger than 250 workers. There were some places where there were more than a thousand people at ASEA. While we had all the major advantages of size, we also had huge disadvantages when it came to tapping the potential of the human mind, growing absenteeism being a good indication. In big companies one doesn't really get the full potential out of people. In contrast, I've seen many alert, fast-moving small companies. Of course, the dream is to combine the two.

What I have tried to do is to recreate small-company dynamism through having five thousand profit centers and thirteen hundred legal entities. I have also made an effort to reduce the layers. I am fully aware, however, of the pros and cons of doing so. Fewer layers means bigger spans of control and fewer jobs to which one can be promoted. But the advantages lie in communication and feedback, or as I call it, "quickback." When you are in the process of change, rapid communication is indispensable.

We try to create an environment where you can have entrepreneurial people, where you can feel engaged, where you do have an overview. Doing this far outweighs the advantages of being able to reduce head count by lumping certain jobs together.

Remember, however, that decentralization is not abdication. You can never say, either at the top or at any point in the hierarchy, "I decentralized this, so that was his fault." You have to be aware of what is going on, and not be afraid to intervene when that is required.

You already touched upon the diseconomies of size. Why bother to keep the group together?

Yes, you can argue, "If you are so fond of small companies, why don't you just spin it all off and divest a thousand companies?" But there are huge advantages in being a large company. You can use common research, you can specialize, you have a better position in dealing with your suppliers in cutting your costs. You can do internal benchmarking, use the best technology, use common distribution channels, and so on.

There are other people in the industry who take another view in the way they run their companies. They will say, "Just let them loose, let them fight it out. Don't worry about the matrix. They don't need a coordinator. People who make the figures will get promoted; the others have to get out." My idea is, if you want to run your business that way, you might as well be separate companies.

By not having global business areas, you do not take advantage of big synergies in R&D, in economy of scale, in distribution, etc.

But what does it mean to have this kind of strategic control over a company the size and complexity of ABB?

Obviously, making our kind of organization work is a lot more demanding. You can mess it up easily. If you have poor business-area managers who don't really achieve the coordination, the system may become clogged. Decisions will be pushed upwards. It is important that within this matrix, you give a clear mandate to the various people in the system. People must have a well-defined role. For example, you can say to a guy at the generator shop in the UK, "You're going to make generators for the whole world up to ten megawatts." Now that is pretty clear. Or, "You will go for these twelve export markets, forget about the others, I will take care of that." If the person coordinating globally has his role clearly spelled out, and the person running a local shop does so as well, they will support each other. When the local company sees the advantage of belonging to a global business area, everything goes more smoothly.

A contrast is often made between ABB and General Electric. How would you compare the two companies? And what can you say about the differences in style between Jack Welch and yourself?

Our businesses are somewhat similar. As far as style is concerned, I think Jack and I are both very execution-oriented. General Electric is still very much an American-based company. Jack comes from a large country with an enormous home market. I am starting from a number of smaller countries, trying to create a global company. However, there are many similarities in the way we approach business.

What is the glue that keeps this gigantic, highly complex organization together?

Well, there are two sorts of glue, the hard and the soft kind. The hard glue is the overall reporting system, ABACUS, that ties together what is going on in the group in a numbers sense. As for the soft kind, that glue is described in what we call our policy bible. That was produced at the inception of ABB and presented at the Cannes meeting. It describes our mission, where we want to be several years from now, and the guidelines for our overall behavior. ABB's values are also concerned with how we should behave internally. To illustrate, one value is that it is better to be roughly right than exactly right, with respect to speed. Then there are rules about minimizing overheads, about integrating newly acquired companies, about rewarding and promoting people.

The most important glue holding our group together is the customer-focus philosophy—how we want to be customer-driven in all respects. The values describe how we want to create a global culture, what can be done to understand each other, the benefits of mixed-nationality teams, and how to avoid being turf defenders. It also includes the basic organizational principles: we want to be flat; we want to be decentralized. Here, I am not talking about empty slogans, but things people can and must adhere to, live by. This is not a glossy brochure with trivial and general statements, but practical advice on how we should treat each other, and the outside world.

It is very nice to put these values in a policy bible, but how do you get people to internalize them?

There are many different ways we can do that. I would say that the most important thing of all, overshadowing everything else, is to live that way yourself. If you say people development is important and then don't develop your own people, you lose credibility. If you talk about speed in action and you procrastinate on certain difficult decisions, you are not believable. So I think that I myself, the members of the executive committee, and [those] further down must "walk the talk," as the Americans say. That's the single most important thing. We must always check that we are living up to what we say. Of course, we have other means, like the large number of seminars we run for our executives. At these seminars, people have an opportunity to discuss how we behave.

You really have to work to get these values internalized. You have to illustrate, sell, and make people buy into these policies.

And if people don't behave according to these policies and break them, you have to be prepared to deal with that too. We can't let people get away with breaking the rules repeatedly. We have to show that we really care about our values.

Some people have commented that your particular kind of organizational design is overdetermined. They refer to your early experiences at home, when your parents were running a printing company.

Yes, there is some truth in that argument. I think we all carry our earlier experiences with us. I grew up in a small family company, a printing shop where ten to fifteen people worked. The workers understood that if they didn't come in on Monday morning, there was going to be trouble. They were really needed. Standing at the printing press, they knew it if a customer got a bad product. So you got a sense of engagement and responsibility in every employee. You won't get the same sense of responsibility in a workshop with a few thousand people. The whole process becomes anonymous. The person becomes a small component in a huge piece of machinery. We have to get out of that kind of situation. Wherever I have gone, at Sandvik, at ASEA, and now at ABB, I have tried to recreate small-company dynamism inside big companies.

What gets you excited at work?

A lot of things. I know I am competitive. Beating the competition for a big project gets me excited, as does breaking into a new industry where we weren't previously. But what really gives me the greatest satisfaction is seeing young people whom I have promoted succeed. Then you have created something that will outlast an individual transaction. At the same time, I have had some of my biggest disappointments when people fail.

How do you manage this continuous process of transformation and change? How do you maintain this kind of momentum? Don't people get tired?

Here, you may see some cultural differences. Americans tend to be quite open to change, even repetitive change. Continental

Europeans are more conservative, while the Scandinavians are somewhere in between. Some people come to me and say, "We have had all these changes: opening Eastern Europe, Asia, these acquisitions. We have doubled our profits. Never in our history have we been at this level of profitability. Can we now have some stability?" Some executives may even feel that I must be mentally ill because I always want more and more. To them, it must seem that I am never satisfied. I can, of course, argue that our profits are not that high by international standards. But given the way I behave, they think I must have some kind of deficiency. They think that I am never satisfied, never happy. Of course, that is not true. I try to explain to people that the world is changing, that our competitors are not standing still. It is like being on an escalator that moves against you. If you stand still you slide backwards; you need to go faster than the escalator to move up. To keep the same jobs and career opportunities, you need to keep a certain momentum. And this continuous setting up of new targets is not unhappiness or ungratefulness about what has been achieved, but it has to be seen as a way of life. They have to get used to the idea that normal life means changes.

I don't think, however, that one should change the organization all the time. There, you need some stability. I want people to focus on the tasks. What will change are higher targets in customer satisfaction, in growth, in profit, and so on. People should ask themselves, "Should I develop new products, penetrate new markets?" They have to constantly test their imagination, their ability to move further. To create this change mentality, you have to show them that the environment, the competitors, the customers are changing. Thus, in order to survive we have to change. You know the expression, "When you are through changing, you are through!"

The question is, how can you continue to rally your forces around certain themes to maintain the momentum? In 1988, we had some painful restructuring. In 1989, we really had to make the new structure work. In 1990, we bought Combustion Engineering; we bought a part of Westinghouse. By doing that, we got a foothold in America. We were the first serious investors in Poland. People were proud of what we were doing in Eastern Europe. And then came the recession, implying recession management—cutting back on people and all that kind of thing. We have used the recession to trim the sails and make ourselves ready for growth. We have our positions in America, in Eastern Europe, and in Asia beyond our traditional strongholds in Europe. Now we have to exploit them. The growth message is giving us momentum again.

After the merger, the revival meeting at Cannes where you got your key managers together created a lot of momentum.

At that time, there was already a missionary feeling. Many people were stunned by the merger. Never in their wildest dreams had they thought that this would happen. Many of them said to themselves, *This is going to hell, this is not going to work.* At Brown Boveri, there had been infighting for a hundred years between Germany, Switzerland, France, and Italy. Other critics of the merger said that the Scandinavians would not fit in continental Europe at all. It was going to be a complete disaster. We were going to prove them wrong; we were going to show them that restructuring across borders could work. The desire among so many of us to prove that the merger would work was an important glue during those first few years.

What do you plan to do to continue this missionary feeling?

To continue the momentum of change, it is important that people in an organization have something to be proud of. It is important that our people can feel pride in something beyond the numbers. For example, if you look at our company now, we have been pioneering investments in Eastern Europe, spearheading East-West integration. I don't want to claim that we knew more than anyone else, but I was absolutely convinced that Eastern Europe would open up. Consequently, because we were the first, we had the pick of the best Polish companies. Many of our people are proud of participating in that process. The same can be said about our work in the environmental field. I would like to create and develop an image of us helping to improve the world environment. For example, transferring sustainable technology to China, or India, where they have a tremendous need to clean up their coal-fired power plants. Our employees can look at work like that and see that we contribute something beyond mere shareholders' value. Internally, we can pride ourselves on certain environmental improvements without being too bombastic or boastful about them. This is particularly relevant for attracting young people to the company. They are by and large not just happy to work for a big company with high profits; they also like to see a purpose that goes beyond numbers. It is important that a company can be perceived as changing the world in a positive way.

When you select people for your global organization, what kind of people are you looking for?

First of all, since we are present in so many countries with such different cultures, I can't say that we have a standard format for a person. Successful individuals in Germany, America, or Italy are all very different. Then there are also different kinds of jobs. There are outgoing, more extroverted jobs, and there are research jobs. That being said, of course we promote the kind of people who live up to our values. The most obvious criteria have to do with success in financial terms. Have you developed your business? If you run a profit center, have you increased your profits?

But beyond that, there is another important question, which is, do you develop your people? Are you a giver, or are you a receiver? The giver makes people available to other parts of the organization; the receiver needs people all the time, be it internally or externally. For me, these are also important criteria.

In addition, to be effective as a global executive you need the ability to understand other people's ways of doing things. You can't—if you come from [for example] America or Scandinavia—look at the Germans and say they are too formal and bureaucratic. They have their own way of operating, which has been very effective. Similarly, you can't look at the way the East Asians do their business and say it's very strange and unusual and not really proper. You just have to understand that things can be done in different ways.

One of the ways to achieve this kind of mind-set, to create global managers, is to send them out to assignments abroad early. For example, we have Americans who have just returned to Ohio after having spent some years in Asia or Europe. They have gotten to know people; they were not just on a business trip. They have worked in these places for some years. Now they understand the global situation better. You have to make them see the benefits of making these exchanges for their own business.

In all this, we must not forget the language problem. English is the official language at ABB, and those who do not speak it must learn to do so. We spend a lot on English language training, for Poles, Mexicans, and so on. Consequently, the majority of people in this organization speak a foreign language. Because of that, we have to be patient. We may all think that we are brilliant in English until we meet an Englishman or an American who thinks that our accents are funny. Many things get lost in the process because of this problem with language. So we have to be patient and give people time to talk and explain themselves.

How do you manage these "high flyers," these global managers?

The fact that we are so few at the head office doesn't mean that we don't keep track of some five to six hundred people who fall into this group. These people are assessed annually by the regional boss and the business-area manager. Personally, I am very much involved in this process. We look at their performance, what they have achieved, whether they have developed their business, the way they interact globally, whether they have developed the people under them. I want to know how many people in the person's organization have made internal moves. One of the most important criteria is whether the person under review can really offer other managerial candidates from his own organization. Thus a person's career is not only measured by the bottom line, but also how the person contributes to group development.

Probably a good example of global executives are the members of the executive committee. How do you complement each other?

We are a very mixed group on the executive committee. We have different nationalities, very different backgrounds. I came out of computer science and business administration; others come from research, marketing, and manufacturing. We have mechanical and electrical engineers. We are American, Danish, Swedish, Swiss, and

German. Five nationalities among eight people. I think it is important to have these different backgrounds and different cultures to
have a broad understanding of the global issues. Sometimes you
hear people complain about lack of the right "chemistry." But
there is no way you can expect the chemistry to be very good everywhere. One has to learn to live with different chemistries in our
organization.

How do you communicate with and motivate people?

A key concern for me is, how do you reach deep down with communication and establish two-way communication? I used to say
that 5 or 10 percent of management is strategic thinking, 90 to 95
percent is execution. A large part of execution is communication,
motivating people and making them buy in, be committed. In our
case we must communicate with twenty-five thousand managers,
who in turn must communicate with everybody else in the organization. That is a gigantic task. In doing so, we always cheat ourselves
at the top. We think that we have made a major resolution, certain
memos have gone out, a reorganization has taken place. But we
have only touched the surface of this huge organization. Lots of
people haven't even heard about our plan of action; they don't care
about it; they don't understand it. So the magnitude of reaching
down, communicating, converting, and influencing people is enormous. One has to be humble when confronted with that task.

There is a tremendous potential in our people that is not
exploited. We haven't talked much about the workers. They only
use 5 to 10 percent of their brain capacity standing at a machine.
Then they go home. There they administer; they organize for the
children; they build a summer house. All of a sudden, they seem
to be able to do an enormous amount of things. Ninety to 95 percent of their brain is now at work. Now, why can't we move these
people into bigger tasks?

We are now experimenting with cutting out a whole layer of
clerical supervision to give teams of workers bigger responsibility. I
think there is a huge potential here that we haven't tapped yet.
This goes deep down to the roots of the way we run industrial organizations. It all comes out of the Taylor system: managers do the

thinking and the workers do the working. This attitude has to be changed. One doesn't need a blue-collar or a white-collar union. We are all in the same boat. When you open up that vista, all of a sudden there is a whole new avenue for exploiting and developing human potential. Future leaders should be able to stimulate and develop this extra capacity inside their companies to be really successful. However, this type of fundamental change in industrial organizations will take a long time to implement—maybe a generation. Those who start early will also reap the benefits early.

Can you say something about yourself, your way of working?

To a large extent I spend my time interacting with people, mainly internal people but also customers. There are probably a few hundred people I talk to and telephone from time to time. I keep a pretty large part of the calendar open so that I'm able to deal with upcoming matters.

People create a certain picture of me, about my capacity for work. True enough, I can work extremely hard for certain periods of time. A good example was during the time of the merger. But I can also take time off. In our company, however, it is not a prerequisite to be a maniac, to be a robot working all the time. People need to have families; they need to have hobbies, they need to have children. I have three children myself. If you're not a whole person who can handle a whole life, you're not a good leader either.

Given your reputation of always being overprepared, do people in the company question some of your ideas? Do they dare to disagree?

It is a difficult question to answer because all executives say, "Oh sure, others disagree." Even the worst dictators tend to say that because they imagine it is like that. Now, I appreciate that my characteristics are sometimes a little bit dominant. At times I can overwhelm people. I'm aware of the risk, sitting in my position, of not getting enough feedback and having a sufficiently open attitude. Of course, it is comfortable, whatever position you are in, to have people agree with you. The temptation is always there. I remember once—without using names—a comment from one of my executives, describing the atmosphere in a particular ABB company. Apparently, if someone disagreed with the president of that company, the person was sure to be fired. When I talked to this elderly president—he is no longer with us—and asked him what would he do if someone under him really objected to what he said, the response was that he would fire him. He didn't try to pretend otherwise. He felt it was natural to act in such a way. If someone went against him, he got rid of the person.

In this organization, for people who know me well there is absolutely no hesitation about saying, "You are wrong. I disagree." But of course in an organization of this size there are many people who don't know me that well. In the Latin countries especially, and maybe in Germany, there is a tendency to be a little cautious, not to offend the top guy. It is a problem to make people really speak their mind and tell you things openly, particularly unpleasant things. I can only say that I am aware of the problem, that I work at it. With new people whom I don't know well, I go out of my way to try to build their confidence so that they don't worry about that aspect of the conversation. How successful I am in doing that is another matter.

In our organization, with all these different cultures and our global presence, we really have no choice but to create an attitude and an atmosphere where people can speak their minds. When people don't come out with real objections to certain decisions, it can be catastrophic for us. It is a must. That doesn't mean that one can do whatever one likes. Once a decision is taken, we demand that people stand behind it whether they like it or not. We don't want them to sabotage it. But before decisions are taken, people must speak their minds!

Of course, the worst thing you can do when you are trying to create an open atmosphere is to interrupt someone, to be degrading, to show your disapproval. Rather, you have to do the opposite. You have to say, "That's a very interesting point," or whatever. You have to bear in mind all the time that you must encourage dissenters. You must demonstrate that willingness. Even when someone goes against you, it should not rebound on them in any way. People shouldn't get the impression that doing so is bad for their career.

What drives you?

What gives me a sense of reward is to create something, to make some kind of lasting impact. Things like penetrating new countries, developing and commercializing new technologies, creating new opportunities. I don't work for the money and the prestige and all that. I guess it is like a person designing a house. People want to build something, create something that is worthwhile. That is what it all boils down to.

What do you see as your personal strengths and weaknesses?

I think someone else had better talk about my strengths, but regarding my weaknesses, I think I sometimes tend to be impatient. Particularly when dealing with people from other cultures who speak slowly, or express themselves slowly, I sometimes make the mistake of being too quick. So there I lose out occasionally in my dialogue with people. I also think, since I am pretty fast, that I sometimes scare people. Consequently, they do not discuss their problems openly, because they feel I know more than they do. Because of my dominance, I may subdue people in a discussion.

What do you dislike most about your work? What causes sleepless nights?

I very rarely have sleepless nights. I am one of those people who can sleep almost anywhere, anytime. For example, if you put a mattress down here in this room, I would be able to sleep instantly. But if you mean what worries me, certainly there are a number of things.

The most unpleasant part of the job is to have conversations with people who have failed—to tell them that they are not up to the requirements of the job. However well you try to handle that process, whatever you do to be caring and have empathy with these people, it is often very tough.

If I look back some years, one very painful thing was this cross-border restructuring of companies at the beginning of the merger, the closing down of plants. While the process is necessary, it may to some extent wear you down. The decisions are highly visible; it becomes a very emotional matter. I remember when we closed a

Swedish semiconductor plant. Although it amounted to only a few hundred people, the plant was the pride of ASEA Sweden, it being high technology. We merged the company with a Swiss one and relocated it here in Switzerland. It was a very traumatic process. Former high-level ASEA officials wrote me letters; they pleaded with me. Some of them were in tears, not just because they had lost their jobs, but because they felt that they had lost out in Sweden. "Please, don't destroy ASEA Sweden. We have been around for a hundred years." There was no limit to how they painted the disaster. I'm talking about two hundred people here; it was heartache. There were demonstrations with torches, marches to the mayor's office. When I came to the city, I was met by demonstrators at the airport. They couldn't believe I could do this to them. This type of thing is not easy to deal with. When you have to close down something, lay off people—even if you have a personnel policy to handle this well and try to offer other jobs and so on—the consequences are very difficult for the people and for the community. It was quite tough and troublesome, even though this decision was right for the group. Sweden was the winner in some other cases when plants were closed elsewhere.

The same thing happened in Switzerland in 1988–89, involving the jobs of three thousand people. I had to convince the Germans and the Swiss that it would be good for the company in the long run. But of course my credibility was not high in the beginning. At the time, some of my close colleagues were emotionally charged up; there were a number who couldn't handle it and they had to be removed because they couldn't execute the change.

In each case there were issues of national pride, particularly when it came to technology. It is hard to believe that an engineer can be so emotionally attached to certain things. It is really like taking a child away, a kind of family disaster. Some were crying—and not because they were thrown out personally. There were some unbelievable stories.

When I came to ASEA, I had to close down a steel plant which was losing SKr100 million per year. My predecessor had invested in a new blast furnace. But it was in the wrong location; it was too small, and its technology was quickly becoming outdated. It was an absolutely dead-end situation. They were not used to that at ASEA in Sweden. On the wall, they had a sign stating that they had not fired anybody in fifty years. And then there comes this maverick who takes this kind of action. Trainloads of people went to lobby the Swedish parliament. It became a big, national issue. I had to have protection for a while. There were all types of threats. My children had a tough time at school. Because I really closed down a town. Four hundred jobs were lost. I did succeed later in bringing back in some hundred and fifty jobs to that community. But these kinds of situations are really painful. They tend to grind you down.

What is difficult here is to combine empathy with decisiveness. You have to go on living. Limit sleepless nights, remorsefulness, and all that. Now, I had a hell of a reputation in Sweden and in Germany. I was called a sort of raider. What I was doing was described as the "Thirty Years War revisited" and the like. I was described as the sort of ruthless person who gets satisfaction out of getting rid of people. The newspapers described it as "Percy's reign of terror." When you do these kinds of things, people think that you are a ruthless character, that you really don't give a damn. But it is a job you have to do. I think good managers do that job well. Napoleon used to say that the best generals are the generals of retreat. The offensive generals are the ones who become famous, but to be able to handle a retreat is something which is often underestimated.

I also think it is important to go out of your way to deal with the people issues in these situations, the families, the financial side of it. But to do that without compromising what you have to do in the end can be difficult.

I feel a little ill when I see this kind of macho thing among some American executives, like the list of the toughest executives in North America. For example, I recall a recent statement by one CEO who said, "From time to time, you have to shoot someone in the courtyard." Who do you impress by that?

If I have someone who has to do this type of work, and he is a pretty ruthless, unemotional character, I think he is not suitable for the job. You asked me what is difficult. This is something that will really grind you down. Fortunately, it is not a thing you do everyday. I have the advantage now, when I deal with other people who have to do it, that I know how it feels. I have done it personally, physically, with my own hands.

During the merger of ASEA and Brown Boveri, you also went through a very difficult period making decisions about which executives would get which jobs. How did you go about it?

During that period, I personally interviewed five hundred people. I didn't know two hundred fifty of them. We had three months to do that kind of thing. It was a very stressful time. What complicated the matter was that the Brown Boveri manager did not necessarily have the same values that we had. To help in selection, we tried to find out certain facts about what these people had actually done. We had at least three people interview each person, and my colleagues also worked extremely hard. I lived for almost two months in a hotel in Baden, Switzerland. I would interview people seven days a week, sometimes twelve to fourteen hours per day, one person after another. It was a crazy period.

It was so important that we not make too many mistakes in these first assignments. A mistake could really hurt the company. So I said to myself, *If ever in my life I have to work like a madman, it should be now.* To make the merger fly, we needed a reasonably good batting average with the people we selected. I knew the ASEA people well, but I didn't know the Brown Boveri ones. Often, it would have been easier to pick an ASEA person because I knew he would perform. But that of course was not acceptable. I really had to take chances on people although I couldn't be certain of how they would perform. That was an extremely active period. I hope I won't have to go through that again.

If a graduating student or a young executive should ask you for advice about how to manage his or her career, what would you say?

I would tell him to be very careful in selecting the executive he is going to work for. The critical thing is to look for a company where they really develop people. That is going to be more important than making, to begin with, two or three thousand kroner more per month. Then the second thing is to do a good job where you are. Also, be yourself. Don't try to imitate or be someone else. All these management books talk about this or that famous person . . . you have to build on your *own* strengths, and your *own* ability.

Could you say something about what the leader of the future should look like?

I don't really believe all that much in the fashion of the seventies leader, the eighties leader, or the nineties leader. When I look back at myself, I think I have been the same kind of leader all along. Like you wear the same old clothes. I can't say if the leader of the 1990s is so very different. Whatever the case may be, leaders have to provide a vision to people, a sense of direction, and a pride in the company. You also need to have the kinds of executives who are able to select good people, stimulate them, and motivate them.

When you are ready to retire, what would you like to be remembered for?

An important thing would be, long after I have left, to see the company develop along its mission. And that we had put into place an organization and people who can continue this development. That's probably the ultimate proof of what one has achieved!

KEY POINTS

ABB's Unique Competitive Edge:

Global organization with deep local roots

- Corporate culture
  - Shared values as "glue," codified in corporate bible.
  - Priority given to accomplishments "beyond the numbers."
  - Responsibility, integrity, trust.
  - Delegation is not abdication.
  - Generativity: mentoring of younger executives.
- Leadership style
  - Walk the talk.
  - Open communication to avoid spread of rumors, discontent.
  - Encourage dissenters.
  - Pragmatic idealism: employment in developing countries, cleaning up the environment.
- Organizational design
  - Small units empower people and foster innovation; inverse relationship between company size and employee motivation; reduce bureaucracy.
  - Ideas and creativity from inside the company; encourage people to use their whole brain at work.
  - Speed: it's better to be roughly right than exactly wrong.
- Continuous transformation and change
  - Shift responsibilities around at all levels of the organization.
  - Set continuous "stretch" goals.
  - Benchmark with the best.
- Building a global organization
  - "Cultural salad" at all levels of the organization.
  - Move young executives around the world.
  - Global operation with deep local roots.
  - Cultural relativity: build on strong points of different cultures, but at the same time push the limits of culture to find opportunities to innovate.

⊕ PART THREE

David Simon

CHAPTER SEVEN

David Simon
The Transformer

Twenty-four hours after the Labour party's landslide victory in the British general election in May 1997, the *Financial Times* mentioned almost as a by-the-way comment that Sir David Simon, chairman of British Petroleum, was to be offered the position of minister for Europe and a seat in the House of Lords. The rumor was pounced on by the pro-Tory press, clearly eager to exploit what looked like an early breach in Prime Minister Tony Blair's cabinet, when the newly appointed foreign secretary, Robin Cook, reacted with fury to the *Financial Times* article—the first he had heard of Sir David's alleged appointment. He had, according to the *Daily Telegraph,* "gone ballistic" over an arrangement that had been made in secret with Blair and about which he had not been consulted. Downing Street responded with an instant denial (yes, Sir David had been consulted generally about European affairs, but "no ministerial post had ever been discussed"; Mr. Cook and Mr. Blair were talking; somebody else entirely would get the job), and the matter died away.

Then a week later it was announced that Sir David Simon was to become minister for European trade and competitiveness, a rather quirkish title for a post that would not, after all, answer to the Foreign Office but would float between the department of trade and industry and the treasury. Sir David, soon to become Lord Simon of Highbury and a member of the House of Lords, announced that he would step down as chairman of BP and waive his ministerial salary of £31,125. As this represented a pittance compared to a salary of £1.2 million (chairman's pay of £241,000 plus benefits), another flurry of headlines followed. BP simultaneously announced that the new nonexecutive chairman of the board would be Peter Sutherland. Sutherland is chairman of Goldman Sachs International and had been deputy chairman of BP since July 1995. John Browne would continue to be the CEO of BP.

Salary considerations alone would be enough to stimulate inquiry into Simon's reasons for leaving BP, but his move raises more intriguing questions than that, not least of which is what prompts somebody to leave a business and a company in which he has worked without interruption for thirty-seven years—moreover, for a political role for which it would appear he has little preparation.

In fact, David Simon's enthusiasm for Europe is long-standing; his status as an authority on European affairs was acquiring concrete form for several years. He is on the board of the Deutsche Bank and has served on the European Commission's competitiveness advisory group. Political and business observers regard Blair's success in tempting him away from BP as a particularly smart move: "David is one of the very few businessmen who have credibility within Europe and with business here. Labour has worked hard to establish credible links with industry but the worry was the ability to deliver. Getting someone of David's reputation is a coup."[1] Although his appointment has been accompanied by warnings about the low success rate among businessmen entering politics, the general feeling seems to be that if anyone can do it, David Simon can. Greater surprise seems to be reserved for his readiness to work for a Labour government. As a believer in the free market, Simon was known to be more of an admirer of Mrs. Thatcher's policies. It had been written of Simon that he had about him

> something of the John Major: the same sober-suited, heavy-spectacled, bank manager exterior, the same good humor masking a more steely edge. . . . The parallels do not end there. Like Mr. Major, Mr. Simon was a bit player in his predecessor's downfall, but once the dagger had been wielded, he found himself thrust to the fore. Both inherited a ship that had been blown off course, both were brought in to mend relations within and outside their organizations, both promised a more collegiate style of management. Both also promised a change of style, rather than of substance. Both, too, moved quickly to jettison some of their former leaders' cherished dogmas.[2]

However, Sir David's style fits well with the values of Blair's New Labour, and his actions accord with the prime minister's now-notorious "people's" rhetoric. Indeed, as the following case study shows, Simon might well be described as "the people's CEO." His attitude is determinedly democratic: when he became chief executive of BP, "Simon sold the corporate jets, closed the executive dining room, and . . . chose to walk to work instead of using a chauffeured car."[3]

David Simon has, like Percy Barnevik, a penchant for dramatic career changes. As the interview reveals, Simon has always been open to opportunities for change, rating these decisions as the most important he has taken. It could be considered that, having become chairman of BP when he did, his opportunities within the company were immediately constricted. After all, when you have reached the top of one of the top companies in the world, there are very few similar peaks left to scale within the same business. You have to look for another mountain in another range. This is what Simon, like Barnevik, has done.

The transition from "Simon's BP" to "Browne's BP" has been a smooth one. Browne, known at BP as a numbers man, has shown that he is capable of maintaining the innovative energy and team feeling that Simon instilled during the transformation process at BP. By emphasizing the importance of continuous learning, he is ensuring that BP employees stay motivated and excited about the future of BP.

ABOUT THE CASE

The BP case study first looks at the difference in leadership styles between David Simon and his predecessor Robert Horton in the context of the upheaval of the oil industry over the past twenty-five years, and the roles the two leaders played in the transformation process at BP. It examines the reasons why, although the two men's goals were nearly identical, their individual style determined failure for one and success for the other. The case addresses issues of transformation and national and corporate cultures in a transnational organization.

When Simon took over as chief executive of British Petroleum in 1992, it had a bloated bureaucracy, was heavily in debt, and was losing money. Since then, BP has become one of the world's most profitable oil companies. His transformational leadership style proved to be a key factor behind the successful turnaround of the organization.

Both Simon and Horton had a similar vision for BP. The latter designed a transformation program modeled after Jack Welch's change process at GE. However, Horton failed to realize that the American leadership style that had served him well in the United States was not at all appropriate for the CEO of BP's global organization. Horton was disliked and mistrusted for what British colleagues and subordinates saw as his abrasiveness and power-hoarding. He was finally ousted in a boardroom coup in 1992. Simon, on the other hand—a man with a great degree of emotional intelligence and cross-cultural sensitivity—won the respect of employees and stockholders alike. He inspired trust, which is essential in a leader taking his organization through a major transformation process.

The time frame of the case covers Simon's five very successful years as CEO, and then chairman, of British Petroleum. Along with the new CEO, John Browne, Simon planned for the future, building on the transformation that has taken place. The interview also looks at BP under John Browne, a leader with a different style, faced with a different task: consolidating and building upon the changes that were made under Simon.

The best leaders of transformation processes are those who get the most out of their subordinates by convincing them that exceptional performance and commitment from everybody involved in the process is ultimately in their *own* self-interest. As the case study shows, no matter how well the change program is designed, it does not succeed if the employees are not behind it.

This is the type of leadership at which Simon excels. He was able to satisfy his followers' needs, and they in turn were willing to comply with his demands. He was able to break the cycle of organizational paralysis and tension that had begun insidiously in the late 1970s and worsened under Horton.

Simon is known for his friendliness and affability. He wanders around and talks to people at all levels within BP, even while in the lavatory. He comes from a middle-class background and is an avid football fan, which provides an important link with different social strata in class-conscious England. He is, as we have already commented, also quite culturally sensitive. By contrast, Horton's lack of cultural sensitivity, and his reputation for abrasiveness and superiority, started the sequence of events that led to his downfall.

Emotional intelligence is as important in a leader as sharp intellect. Briefly, emotionally intelligent individuals are able to recognize their own emotions and the reasons behind them. They are able to manage these emotions by controlling or finding appropriate outlets for them. They use their emotions to motivate themselves to accomplish goals. Leaders with these qualities are more effective because they are in turn able to empathize with and appropriately channel their subordinates' emotions as well. These qualities are obviously essential during a transformation process.

In addition, Simon's image as an accessible group leader engendered honest, focused, and persuasive communication. This aspect of leadership has also been described as the teddy bear factor, meaning the leader becomes an emotional "container" for employees' hopes and anxieties and thereby creates a positive, safe environment.[4] Leaders with a teddy bear image have the emotional intelligence to provide a sense of security for followers. Simon let employees know that they were being listened to. These processes were responsible for the kind of stretch and high motivation that drove employees toward a successful change effort. These are key factors that allowed Simon to create a facilitating environment for change—something that Horton, despite his technically feasible *OPEN* program (which Simon later implemented practically unaltered; the program is discussed in Chapter Eight), was unable to do.

This teddy bear effect can be explained by the fact that, on an unconscious level, followers tend to identify with their leaders (through a transferential process called *idealizing*) and project on them their hopes for a new alternative. Thus followers try to please their leaders by making things happen for them. Leaders gain strength from this mutual identification process and then reassure their followers, who in turn assure the leaders of their support.

Once you have read the case in Chapter Eight and the interview that follows in Chapter Nine, it might be interesting to reflect on the different personal styles of the leaders featured in this book. Which would you feel most comfortable working with? The Swedish alchemist who finds national and cultural boundaries no barrier to successful business relationships? The eternal Peter Pan who works so hard at taking his people on adventures and having fun? Or the teddy bear who does not hesitate, when necessary, to show his teeth?

CHAPTER EIGHT

Transformational Leadership at British Petroleum

THE REIGN OF ROBERT HORTON

On June 25, 1992, Robert Horton, chairman and CEO of British Petroleum, was ousted after only two years at the helm. His fall from grace was precipitous, surprising even senior management. Lord Ashburton, who later took Horton's place as chairman, and the other nonexecutive members of the board had had doubts about Horton for some time, however. It was those niggling doubts, rather than a specific event, that prompted the directors to act. "It was an accumulation of feelings, of events, all quite small in themselves," Ashburton explained. "We felt the company would be better organized if we had a change of individual."[1] Horton agreed to resign, thus ending his thirty-five-year career with BP.

ROBERT HORTON IN THE UNITED STATES, 1986–1990

It is reported that while still at university Robert Horton predicted he would become CEO of BP. In 1957, he joined the company as an engineering trainee, beginning his steady rise through the

117

organization. In 1986, having worked his way up through the ranks, he was appointed by then-CEO Sir Peter Walters to head Standard Oil in Cleveland, Ohio. In 1987, BP bought the 45 percent of Standard Oil that it did not already own and, with BP's other North American holdings, formed BP America. Horton was named CEO of the new organization.

Proving to be adaptable and street-smart, he transformed his image from a feared Brit whose reputation as "Horton the Hatchet" (after his method of reducing losses by cutting the workforce) had preceded him to a trusted and respected insider. He "Americanized" himself, becoming popular on the Cleveland social circuit, joining Sen. Robert Dole's 1988 campaign for the U.S. presidency, and even contemplating running for a seat in the U.S. Senate himself. He explained that his liking for Americans began as a small boy during World War II, when American pilots were quartered with his family. They always seemed to have chewing gum or loose change in their pockets for young Robert. He remembers that time as "great fun."

Though he was brutally honest about the necessity for personnel cuts when he arrived at Standard Oil, he was able to convince employees that the strategy made sense. Horton explained: "It's what an executive has to do. It's a matter of persuading people that however bad the news, the result is going to be better for them. I wanted employees to know that my mission was to help the company recover, not to go around smashing things up."[2]

He set up and attended more than fifty "town meetings" at BP divisions across America, saying he wanted employees to see that he did not have horns and a tail. During his tenure, Horton restored morale and kept it high even through extensive corporate change. He also reduced BP America's self-image of a colonial outpost by making the symbolic gesture, at Cleveland headquarters, of hanging there the first and only portrait of Standard Oil founder John D. Rockefeller.

When Horton was named BP's CEO in September 1989, the Cleveland locals were sorry to see him go. Cleveland's mayor described Horton as a role model for responsible corporate executives, and the chamber of commerce elected him as the city's outstanding business executive for that year.

ROBERT HORTON IN ENGLAND, 1990–1992

Once back on the British side of the Atlantic, Horton made it clear that his ties to America would continue. The following comments appeared in the *Wall Street Journal* in 1989:

> *Horton Seeks an American Accent for BP*
>
> The heir apparent of British Petroleum Co. wants to Americanize Britain's biggest company. Mr. Horton, an unusually brash Briton enamored of the U.S., will bring a much more American flavor to BP. . . . "BP is, in a funny sense, more of an American company than a British company," he says. . . .
>
> Robert Horton's track record for diplomacy could prove crucial as he Americanizes BP. . . . Last spring, Horton rejoined BP's governing board in London, where he began bringing more Americans into headquarters jobs and forging the corporate-identity drive. He isn't satisfied. BP, he says, should "at least double" its proportion of U.S. stockholders. . . .
>
> Mr. Horton intends to visit the U.S. every six weeks—a pattern which differs markedly from Sir Peter's twice-yearly visits. "You just have to work at being visible," says Mr. Horton, one leg casually draped over a green leather armchair in his 31st floor London office. . . .[3]

BRITISH PETROLEUM AND THE GLOBAL OIL INDUSTRY, 1980–1992

Once settled into his new office, Horton had to turn his attention to some pressing problems. Many of them were endemic to the world's major oil companies at that time and were not new. Until the early 1980s, the oil majors had been unusually centralized for organizations of comparable size. This was a result of the interdependent nature of the oil production business: there was close interaction vertically among exploration, production, refining, and marketing; and horizontally among the end products.

The oil crises of 1973–74 and 1979–80, however, provoked a transition from a postwar period of growth and stability to one of stagnation, volatile commodity prices, and accelerated technological change. Although the management systems in place to control the industry were growing increasingly inefficient in the face of the fast-moving external environment, oil executives focused their energy on making do, rather than maximizing assets.

As the market environment changed, the widening gap between the organizations' strategy and the external demands caused performance to decline. Still, most major oil companies maintained existing structures and strategies, seeking to boost profitability and shareholder return through diversification. BP, for example, acquired interests in animal feeds, underwater surveying, plastics, computer systems, and tin production, among other things.

Unfortunately, new assets did not prove to be the panacea for the industry. In 1981, British Petroleum was the first oil major to announce a "redefinition of divisions and increased divisional autonomy"—at a time, not coincidentally, when it was suffering a decline in profitability. This restructuring process initiated an abrupt reversal in BP's diversification strategy, mainly because the periphery businesses had failed to contribute shareholder value— still the primary goal of the company. BP moved back to its core interest, petroleum. In BP's 1988 annual report, then-CEO Peter Walters said: "With our strategic criteria, we continually review all of BP's activities, hydrocarbon-based or otherwise. If certain operations are worth more than others to ourselves, or if they no longer fulfill our requirements and show little prospect of doing so, we are prepared to sell them."[4]

Another fundamental strategic change was cost reduction; lower costs would equal increased profitability. BP executives began to focus on economies of scale (larger refineries and tankers) and maximizing technological advances to improve productivity. In addition, all the oil majors made strenuous efforts to reduce administrative costs.

Most important, the oil companies were beginning to recognize the need for a dramatic change in corporate culture. As the British *Journal of Management* explained in a history of the industry's restructuring, "The changes in strategy and organizational structures [in the oil industry in the 1980s] had the effect of profoundly dislocating the corporate cultures which had been built up by the companies during their 'administrative bureaucracy' eras. . . . As a result, the companies represented fertile ground for the implantation of new values and new behavioral norms. Management of corporate culture involved two main objectives. The first was to reinforce the structural changes intended to encourage responsiveness and flexibility by instilling the values of entrepreneurship and individual initiative. . . . The second was improving integration through a unity of values and goals."[5]

A vision statement along these lines was circulated throughout BP in March 1990: "We believe in continually developing a style and climate which liberates the talents, enthusiasm and commitment of all our people. We can then respond positively to the increasing pace of change in a rapid and flexible way to achieve real competitive advantage."[6]

Decentralization was imperative if the company was to attain these lofty goals. Although BP had made a first attempt at creating a flatter organization through matrix structure in the late 1980s, this new system ended up creating more bureaucracy. Paradoxically, it became more *centralized* as the matrix structure led to "constipation" in decision making. BP's top managers were increasingly overburdened, spending most of their time traveling and in meetings, just trying to keep up with daily operations in each major business and in each country. All problems, small or great, were referred to London headquarters. Information was spread through standard notices—with the same notice sent to all interested parties, from top management to outside journalists.

This created a great amount of confusion. An opinion survey, conducted just after Horton's arrival, revealed that half of the 150 senior staff managers polled were unsure of what BP's five-year strategy and mission were. They also said that BP's structure lacked operational flexibility and collaboration. This criticism came up again in another survey of four thousand employees conducted several months later.

PROJECT 1990

Observers welcomed Horton's arrival and thought that BP would benefit from his ability to take charge rapidly and his experience in instituting change. One of his first actions as CEO was to announce that BP would have to go through "the corporate equivalent of *perestroika* and *glasnost*."[7] He initiated Project 1990, a research-and-consultation process patterned after similar projects in America, which was to prepare the company for major transformation. Briefly, the goals of Project 1990 were to understand the old as well as the present culture at BP, transform the prevailing "civil service" mentality, and create a new culture based on *OPEN:* "*O*pen thinking, *P*ersonal impact, *E*mpowering, and *N*etworking." The organization's vision statement was unequivocal: "With our bold, innovative strategic agenda, BP will be the world's most successful oil company in the 1990s and beyond."[8]

The objectives of the transformation were both hard and soft. BP's hierarchical, bureaucratic structure would be replaced with a flatter organization, leading to reductions in head office staff. But Horton also realized that the corporate culture would have to change to make the new structure work. He wanted to get rid of the stuffiness, power hoarding, and atmosphere of distrust.

Several key executives supported Project 1990 publicly. One of them was David Simon, who had been Horton's rival for the CEO position in 1989 (and who would soon take Horton's place). Simon emphasized repeatedly his commitment to Project 1990. He said that although people might expect him to be the rock on which the culture change would founder, he would actually be one of the rocks on which it would be built (a reference to Christ's disciple Simon Peter).

Over the next year, senior managers met around conference tables to debate and implement Project 1990's radical proposals for changing the company. The meetings grew more and more informal, positive, and open. People began to express their real opinions.

However, after this good start, the process began to bog down. An internal survey in 1991 revealed that many employees were disillusioned with the program. It was felt that Horton was *imposing* change rather than *fostering* it.

To make matters worse, in 1992 BP's financial situation went from satisfactory to dismal: profits were down by 85 percent from the previous year, and the company's debt-to-equity ratio rose to 81 percent by March 1992. The company cited market fluctuations because of the Gulf War as one reason for its difficulties. In fact, a major problem was BP's decision to continue high investment through a recession that was stubbornly slow to end.

In response, Horton began another round of cost cutting, which in turn exacerbated the severe morale problem at BP. Project 1990 soon became a euphemism for downsizing—and thereby lost its effectiveness in transforming corporate culture. One executive recalls seeing issues of BP's internal magazine, *Oil,* that had page after glossy page of upbeat news, while never mentioning that thousands of BP employees were being laid off.

Horton was correct in realizing that change was overdue, but he erred in insisting that it be done his way. He made the mistake of forcing employees to accept the changes at BP without clearly communicating the reasons and goals behind the process. Many people found fault with Horton for expecting others to empower their subordinates and work on trust and teamwork while he himself—as they saw it—failed to give up any personal power or trust anyone else's judgment as much as his own.

In addition, consensus had it that although Horton's management style may have worked in America, it produced little more than resentment in BP's more conservative British headquarters. In an interview that appeared in *Forbes* in February 1992, Horton said: "Because I am blessed with my good brain, I tend to get to the right answer rather quicker and more often than most people. That will sound frightfully arrogant, but it's true. So I have to rein in my impatience."[9]

The *Forbes* interviewer closed by saying that Horton sounded as if he had "precisely the mix of self-confidence and personal discipline required to run effectively an organization as sprawling and complex as BP." The interview did not go down at all well in England, however, where British readers found his remarks to be appallingly self-aggrandizing.

As a result of all these problems, the nonexecutive directors took action. With the compliance of the executive directors, the board informed Horton that BP needed a change at the top. On June 25, 1992, he resigned from his position of chairman and CEO of BP and was replaced by Lord Ashburton as chairman and David Simon as CEO.

In the analysis that followed Horton's resignation, one journalist described the situation in an understatement: "Horton's experience in the U.S. reinforced his natural penchant for a high-profile leadership style, the virtues of which include more openness and plain-speaking than is the norm in British business."[10] Since many top executives had supported Horton's Project 1990, it would be inaccurate to say that the project itself was "too American." Rather, it was Horton's leadership style that brought him down. His *style* was too American, and as a result, he never fully gained the trust and respect of his colleagues and subordinates when he returned to London as CEO.

As an interesting aside, one observer pointed out that combining the position of CEO and chairman, as in Horton's case, almost always proves to be a mistake: "With the backing of the right chairman, there is every reason to believe that Horton's considerable talents could have been channeled to successful efficiency and that this latest act of self-mutilation by an important British company could have been avoided."[11]

DAVID SIMON'S RISE TO THE TOP

Simon, Horton's successor, was well suited to be the leader of an Anglo-Saxon organization with an eye on expansion in continental Europe, South America, and Asia. He speaks five languages, among them excellent French and German. He accepted an invitation in 1995 from the president of the European Commission to become a member of the newly formed competitiveness advisory group. He is more European than typically British, in many ways, particularly in his chatty, affable manner. He attributes this to his family background: his father was Welsh and his stepfather French.

Born in England in 1939, Simon lived with his artist mother and grandmother until his mother fell in love with a heroic Free French fighter pilot who had escaped the Nazis and washed up on England's shore in a fishing boat. Simon's mother took her son and followed her new husband to France, where the family lived for two years after the war. The family left France in 1947 and returned to England when the French ousted Charles de Gaulle. Later, in school, Simon found that he could speak French better than anyone else, including the teachers.

He enjoyed school, mainly because of the sports: "What interested me were the folks I met and the games I played. I still haven't got out of the idea that half of life is playing soccer, rugger, tennis, that sort of thing."[12] (He sat on the sports council in England and continues to be an avid fan of Arsenal, a leading London soccer team. His language is sprinkled with sports metaphors. One close colleague reports that he has to keep up with the sports pages just to be able to figure out what Simon is talking about.) Simon was not, however, a natural academic. An important milestone in his life came when a teacher told him that he should consider going into industry, which Simon took to be a diplomatic way of saying that he would never be an intellectual. That teacher also suggested that he apply to BP.

So at the age of eighteen, Simon presented himself, in the same building where he would later preside as chairman, for his first job interview. He was so nervous that after ten minutes he had to leave the room to be sick. "Can you imagine? What an idiot!" says Simon now.[13] Despite this unconventional behavior, his gift for languages appealed to a company that was beginning to focus on expansion in Europe. He was hired as a university intern, meaning that he worked for BP during every long vacation from his studies at Cambridge. His goal at that time was "to make £3 per week last, and to keep enough beer in my system to continue playing rugby with friends."[14] He continued to be an average student at Cambridge, where he studied modern languages, but he enjoyed his stints at BP. After graduation, he went to work at BP full-time in the marketing department.

Though Simon was pegged early on as more of a sporting type, he has always had a drive to succeed. He recounts a revealing anecdote about his time at INSEAD, where he obtained an MBA in 1966: "Not getting a good degree at Cambridge annoyed me intensely, as I thought I was relatively smart. In fact, it really bussed me off, so when it came to the MBA I was absolutely determined academically to do it properly. I knew what I wanted to get out of it. I was really focused and knew if I worked hard, I could get an academic result which would satisfy me."[15]

And he did—he says he "passed out first equal" in his year. He then spent the next ten years working for BP on the Continent. He visited filling stations throughout Europe, gaining grassroots experience and ideas that he would later draw on as CEO. In 1982, he became chief executive of BP Oil International; in 1986, a managing director of the BP Group; and in 1990, chief operating officer of the BP Group. Finally, in 1992, he replaced Horton in the top spot.

DAVID SIMON, CEO, 1992–1995

The situation facing Simon when he took over BP on June 25, 1992, was bleak. The organization needed to drastically revise its business strategy to reverse losses, and it had to repay billions of dollars in debt. Simon moved fast. He implemented a three-year plan with a simple name: "1-2-5." The goals of that plan were to cut debt by $1 billion per year, build annual replacement-cost profits to $2 billion per year, and keep capital spending below $5 billion per year. Over the following two years, he cut costs by selling off more than $6 billion worth of peripheral businesses (including the nutrition group) and by downsizing the workforce by almost 50 percent, with a large reduction in middle management. Head office staff went from 3,000 in 1989 to 380 in 1992, which allowed the company to move to more modest headquarters. Simon also narrowed BP's core interest to petroleum only—"finding it, extracting it, shipping it, refining it, converting it, and selling it,"[16] as he put it—through three main divisions: exploration, oil, and chemicals. Oil production costs were slashed as a result of improved technology.

One of the first goals of the reorganization process was to push decision making down to local levels. Middle managers were made responsible for, and given a financial stake in, the production of their divisions. The underlying management structure was changed to that of a network organization; managers of different divisions began to work more closely with their colleagues, rather than always through superiors. This meant that when a specific technical problem arose, for example, the manager would call a colleague who had dealt with a similar problem in the past, rather than automatically contacting his own boss. Initiative, not conformity, was encouraged.

Simon's focus paid off. In August 1994, he declared that BP's recovery program was nearly complete. The goals of the 1-2-5 strategy had been achieved a year ahead of schedule, which sent stockholder confidence soaring. By early 1996, BP's share price had more than doubled from what it was in 1992, and the organization had better results than its arch rival, Shell, in return on capital.

Simon has said that setting simple goals is an important part of developing a culture of continuous performance improvement. He tells the symbolic story of his visit to a multimillion-dollar oil-drilling platform: "I asked the workers, 'What are you doing?' 'Drilling oil,' they replied. 'How much money are you making?' I asked them. The workers had no idea. I wanted to know how much money they were making there, and they said they could tell me how much oil they produced. I told them I wasn't interested in how much oil they produced. The platform is a factory, for me. Where's the money? That oil is relevant only in terms of money for the shareholders, not in terms of barrels."[17]

Simon made it clear to BP employees that they should be cost- and profit-conscious. He has a golden rule for attaining goals: "Targeting is fundamental to achieving. If you do not target, you do not measure and you do not achieve." He believes that "picking the right targets is a skill in itself. The difficulty of leadership is picking the targets and having a dialogue as you progress towards that goal so that, when it is achieved, it seems the easiest thing in the world. Then you can pick another target."[18]

(Back when Simon was a student at Christ's Hospital, a master told him he would be a "burned-out shell of a man" if he didn't focus. "That is when I learned to pick targets," he says.)[19]

Equally important, Simon addressed the morale problem permeating the organization. Employees describe him as a good communicator who, unlike his predecessor, inspires trust. Influenced by his background in marketing, Simon puts a high emphasis on "people skills." Ironically, he was initially passed over in favor of Horton for the CEO position in 1989 partly because he was seen to lack the latter's proven leadership ability. Insiders say that he is just as tough, though more diplomatic. He is described as "wily, subtle, diplomatic, and knowledgeable about the undercurrents of the British establishment"—an area in which Horton showed little sensitivity. Despite his mild demeanor, he has a mind like a steel trap. "He knows the figures like the night sky," says a colleague, "and that allowed [him] to navigate [his] way through a group as complex as BP." Furthermore, he proved to be good at anticipating issues that no one else had focused on.

Simon was careful to point out that, despite the uproar over Horton's leadership style, continuity of control and direction was one of his own goals when he became CEO in 1992. At that time, he said: "This is about the style of running the company at the top. It is not about changes in strategy."[20] He had been an early and vocal proponent of Project 1990, and though Horton took much of the blame for the painful restructuring, Simon continued with it. (In fact, in March 1996, BP announced that Horton was one of nine present and former BP directors who would share a £10.5 million award as part of the organization's long-term performance-linked bonus plan. According to BP's 1995 annual report, Horton "was able to initiate certain changes . . . which have benefited the performance of the company.")

As one top executive described Simon's accomplishment during his first three years as CEO: "What he has done so well is pull the company together in a very calming way, setting clear targets and telling people how they can achieve them." An outside analyst commented: "I think you have to put an awful lot of BP's recovery down to him. A complete cultural change has been put into place." Another executive said: "It has been a big change in terms of the style and role of the leader. Simon's style is to encourage people to fill the space that he leaves around him. He has a very sophisticated and quite unique talent for guiding people without their really knowing he is doing it."[21]

Some of Simon's worst moments came when he had to tell colleagues that they would not be promoted. "The people decisions are always the toughest," he says. "The business decisions may involve a lot of money, but they're never as hard."[22]

Simon once said that he keeps in mind a friend's advice: "Listen first, think next, and act after."[23] His leadership style: "I like talking through problems; I don't jump to conclusions. I love teamwork."[24] Simon's definition of bad management comes as no surprise: "[Bad managers are] managers who don't listen. Telling is not enough."[25]

Simon emphasizes the importance of personal contact at all levels within the organization. He likes to wander around and talk to people: the secretaries, the drivers, the tea ladies, the people he meets in the corridor or the lavatory. He says that these people have their own network and see life in the organization differently from how those in management do.

Why was Simon successful where Horton was not? Simon recognized that letting go of the old way of doing things is not only a cognitive process; it is first and foremost a sequential emotional process. Corporate change often starts with a state of turmoil. With the anxiety level rising, normal organizational processes generally come to a halt or become ritualistic. People fall back to familiar routines, going through motions they know well as they try to deal with the announced change. This is what happened at BP under Horton.

As a reaction to the shock experienced by what was happening to and around them, many people in the organization reacted to Horton's *OPEN* program with passivity and lack of initiative, or on the other hand, displaced anger or "fight" behavior. Employees made Horton the scapegoat responsible for the organization's problems and became bitter, although many of the problems were beyond the chief's control.

Obviously, this type of behavior could not go on. People became aware of the need for profound change, and the board realized that the lack of astute leadership was a major cause of the turmoil at BP. David Simon proved to have the emotional intelligence necessary to win employees' confidence and lead them through the transformation process.

Observers and insiders alike were amazed by the change in the company after the first painful years of restructuring. BP management has acknowledged that the joint ventures, new businesses, and management realignment were made possible by the atmosphere of democracy that Simon fostered in the company.

THE ASCENT OF JOHN BROWNE

In July 1995, Simon became chairman of BP, leaving his place as CEO to John Browne, former head of BP's exploration division. Though Simon is strong in business acumen, his greatest strength lies in relationship management. When he became chairman, he had the good sense to form a well-balanced leadership dyad with Browne, who has a reputation for being the best "numbers man" at BP.

Browne, who was trained as an engineer, is a dyed-in-the-wool oilman. As the son of a BP man, he spent his childhood abroad.

He was fascinated by oil workers he met as a boy in Iran. "They were interesting and worldly people,"[26] he remembers. He began his career with BP just out of university, working in the oil fields of Alaska. He is known for having turned around BP's oil exploration division in the early 1990s and is widely admired in the business community.

When Browne became CEO, he took the reins of an organization that was in excellent financial shape. "We have clawed our way back,"[27] he said at the time. The company had 53,000 employees, down from 129,000. Previously BP had been called the corporate equivalent of high tea: traditional, formal, and predictable.[28] Now Browne describes BP as "a very flat, team-based organization that is designed to motivate and help people to learn. We've divided the company up into lots of business units, and there is *nothing* between them and the nine-member executive group."[29]

Browne insists on the importance of maintaining a learning culture that allows experimentation, and even mistakes. He feels that learning is the key to adapting to rapidly changing environments; ideas have a "diminishing half-life and we need a constant stream of new thinking if we're going to keep ahead of the competitors."[30] The learning culture is based on systems that foster close interaction among employees, allowing them to get the information they need from each other.

An important tool is BP's virtual team network, a computer network designed to help people share knowledge regardless of time, geographical location, and position in the organization. The virtual network was made available to everyone at BP under one condition: that each department pay for it from their own budget. According to Browne, "They said, 'We don't mind. It's just fantastic.' It's an example of how an organization changes itself when it sees something worthwhile."[31] Browne says that it is this ability to transfer learning from one part of the company to another that makes a global business more than the sum of its parts.

Browne has also installed a process to encourage "breakthrough thinking": when faced with a seemingly unattainable target, assign the best minds to the project, get them working together regardless of where they are located, and force them to broaden their thinking and reanalyze every detail of the problem.

He and Simon described BP's goal as being the best in each of its eleven criteria for business success, from oil exploration to business investment. According to Browne: "What's important to us is that whatever business we're in, we focus on getting a position which is as close to dominating as possible. But we're going to do it in such a way that we don't imperil the financial structure of the company again."[32]

Browne's aim is to create a "distinctive" organization, with elements that competitors would have difficulty copying. He wants to create a unique set of assets, including markets, and wants to provide unusual financial returns to investors.[33] In BP's 1995 annual report, he wrote: "To achieve distinctive performance from a portfolio of first-class assets requires continuous development of our organization and management processes. We are further decentralizing the organization in order to encourage personal initiative and creativity. Simultaneously, we are strengthening the sharing of experience and best practice so that BP's total competitive strength is greater than the sum of its parts."[34]

By *distinctive assets,* Browne means assets that a company has in disproportion to its rivals. He sees giant oil fields and market share as distinctive assets for BP in this sense. Technology also provides distinctiveness, as do BP's relationships with the rest of the world— customers, suppliers, governments, nongovernmental organizations, communities, and so on. BP thinks of the relationships as long-term and based on mutual advantage.

Browne also mentions organization, meaning the *process* by which the company motivates its people and fosters creativity, learning, and sharing know-how. Because these soft management areas are unique to a company and are hard to copy, they add a competitive edge. Distinctive relationships are essential. Employees should be highly motivated, understand what they have to do to create value, see the results of their actions, and feel empowered. "We must view relationships as a coming together that allows us to do something no other two parties could do—something that makes the pie bigger and is to your advantage and to my advantage."[35]

Browne also insists on the importance of communicating *purpose*. "A clear purpose allows a company to focus its learning efforts in order to increase its competitive advantage. . . . Our purpose is who we are and what makes us distinctive. It's . . . what we're will-ing and not willing to do to achieve it. . . . In our pursuit of excep-tional performance and sustained growth, there are certain financial boundaries we will not cross and values we will not vio-late. These values concern ethics, health, safety, and the environ-ment, the way we treat employees, and external relations."[36]

Elsewhere, on the same subject, Browne also says, "[Our employees] have hopes for the world and for their children. And they have fears. . . . Our fundamental goal is to provide the people of the world with the energy they need in a safe and careful way, which means that we aren't sacrificing tomorrow for today."[37]

(When asked what *he* sees as distinctive assets, Simon answered with a twinkle in his eye: "If I told you that, you'd have a piece of information worth zillions! You'll never get a straight answer to a question like *that* from a thinking businessman.")

Browne is aware that BP's strong comeback has been at least partly the result of staff reduction, and he has not forgotten the lessons learned during the painful downsizing that occurred between 1992 and 1995. He will not rule out the possibility of fur-ther cuts in the future, but he does not believe that reduction in personnel should be a long-term strategy: "It's a very complex problem. In a business driven by technology, over time, each per-son becomes more productive. . . . Change for change's sake is not on the agenda."[38]

Simon concurs, saying: "Performance based on ever-improving teamwork is the theme carried forward by the managing directors and the senior management team.[39] I'm always interested to see which people are influential in a team, why a team plays better with some individuals. I'm always trying to understand what makes a football team work, just as I do with a team at the office. You're always trying to work out which is the best mixture—and it's never the six or eight most able people.[40]

Simon's slogan is "performance, reputation, and teamwork"; he believes that you should judge a leader not by his or her indi-vidual performance but by the effectiveness of the leader's team, along with the leader's own ability to be a team player.

As Browne took on the CEO position, Simon once again stressed the importance of continuity. He asserted that BP under Browne would focus on the same key goals: strengthening the balance sheet, developing competitiveness in Europe and the Far East, and achieving "profitable, disciplined growth."

Though he is convinced that shooting for clear targets is essential for progress, Simon is realistic about the shortcomings of this perspective. He says that he sometimes gets overly enthusiastic and impatient when trying to fit things into a model—a trait that he considers to be a weakness.[41] Because he is aware of the dangers of rigidity, he is able to keep his eye on the goal while still remaining flexible.

1996 AND BEYOND

In January 1996, BP announced that it would reduce its worldwide refining capacity by 30 percent, reflecting the company's belief that BP's performance is more important than its size. Simon and Browne acknowledged that, having sold most of its peripheral businesses as well as four refineries, BP had little scope for further cost reduction through sales of assets. Browne said that BP intended to focus on volume growth and competitiveness through continuously better management and exploitation of assets, costs, and productivity, rather than through cost cutting.

Though it is hard to find a critic of this strategy, it is not without risk. For a long time, BP was unusually dependent on a relatively small number of oil and gas fields. (Shell, on the other hand, operates in 130 countries.) Simon's cost-cutting measures from 1991 to 1994 resulted in a drop in upstream investment of $1.5 billion during that period, in part due to improved technology and less wasteful expenditure. By 1994, the company was exploring for oil in far fewer countries. (When the company was founded in 1908, its name—Anglo-Persian, later Anglo-Iranian—reflected its complete dependence on oil-rich fields in the Middle East. The name was changed to British Petroleum in 1954. After the company was booted out of Iran, Libya, and Nigeria—all OPEC member countries—it concentrated on fields in Alaska and the North Sea.)

Today, the lion's share of BP's oil and gas comes from its huge but mature fields in North America and Britain. BP believes that it can replace exhausted fields with new reserves. Exploitation of smaller oil fields, which was not profitable in the past given the exploration and development costs involved, is being made possible through new technology. BP is also venturing into the only large new fields left in the world: those located mainly in areas that are difficult to exploit for political or environmental reasons. Most of the areas in which BP is prospecting—Colombia, Algeria, Venezuela, Vietnam, Azerbaijan, the Gulf of Mexico, Alaska, Norway, and the Shetland Islands—pose difficulties in terms of political instability or technical and environmental risks (such as those inherent in deepwater drilling).

In particular, problems have arisen in Colombia, where guerrillas have increased their attacks against oil exploration and production sites. In August 1996, BP signed a controversial agreement with the Colombian defense ministry that provided for the Colombian army to protect BP's production sites in that country. Such payments are the norm for oil, mining, and other companies operating in remote areas vulnerable to guerrilla attack, but this did not save BP from charges of complicity in human-rights violations by a British member of the European Parliament and several nongovernmental organizations, which accuse Colombia's military of having a deplorable human rights record. BP has defended its $8 million contribution, spread out over three years, as being unavoidable if the company is to secure protection for its staff. It has called upon the independent Colombian prosecutor general to investigate the charges of complicity, which it firmly rejects.

Despite similar risks due to political instability, BP's recent $3 billion natural gas contract in Algeria was designed to give the firm major clout in the international market. This contract is one element of a new phase of growth and capital investment for the company, as it will make BP a major provider to Southern Europe.

Environmental concerns are often a factor. For example, technological advances have made it commercially feasible to extract oil in the Atlantic Ocean west of the Shetland Islands, an area that was previously deemed too difficult to exploit. Unfortunately, this is an environmentally sensitive area. BP has also been criticized for causing environmental damage to its sites in Colombia. Browne admitted to environmental "mistakes" but said that they had been fixed. These and similar problems have led Greenpeace and other environmentalists to focus the public's eye on BP's developments. As Simon said during his tenure as chairman, if there was anything that kept him awake at night it was the environmental issues, which are always a big worry for anyone in the oil business.

On a more positive note, BP made an important strategic move in February 1996 by announcing a partnership with the American oil giant Mobil, to pool their assets—$3.4 billion in BP assets and $1.6 billion from Mobil—in refineries and service stations in Europe. This allows the two companies to emerge as the market leader in six countries (and the second largest oil marketer in Europe), with annual sales of more than $20 billion.[42] The move is expected to save the companies $400–500 million annually. The deal also enables the companies to expand into other markets in the future, particularly in Central and Eastern Europe. Another reason for the deal is the cutthroat competition for markets in Europe: there are too many refineries producing too much gasoline, despite declining demand from the better fuel efficiency of new vehicles and rising fuel taxes. Lucio Noto, Mobil chairman and CEO, said that the deal is a test case that could lead to wider cooperation between the two organizations. "The real issue is to get the two cultures to work together. That will give us a clue to whether we could do more in the future, and how we could do it."[43]

In November 1997, BP announced that it had signed a deal to invest more than $500 million in Russia's fourth largest oil company, and $170 million in Eastern Siberian gas fields. This was an important breakthrough for BP. Western oil companies had been trying to get a foothold in ex-Soviet oil fields since the break up of the USSR, with little success. BP finally found a way in: through buying a share of the country's vast reserves, rather than drilling its own wells. John Browne commented that "access to Russian reserves has been an element of BP's strategy for some time, but we needed to have evidence of a clear economic direction and an environment in which we could be confident of doing business over the long term."[44] Not only does BP stand to profit from the extremely low price per barrel of the Russian oil (though once again there are risks of political instability to consider) but it also gains access to another vast market: China. Supplying gas from these fields to the expanding markets of China and the Far East was one of the topics discussed during Russian president Boris Yeltsin's November 1997 summit with the Chinese president, Jiang Zemin.

According to Browne, these deals are steps in his strategy to build on BP's strengths rather than diversify. Retaining and enlarging market share is in line with BP's other main sources of future growth: attaining higher volumes and margins on production and higher returns on refining and chemical production.

"THE BEST IS YET TO DO"

Given BP's situation when Simon took over in 1992, he undoubtedly made the right choices: focusing on tightening up the operation and maximizing the potential of core industries. Looking back in 1996, he said: "The negative job, of shrinking the business, is often not seen as that marvelous; it is seen as different [from] the job of expanding the business. They have different priorities and different challenges. Personally, I find both extremely challenging and interesting."[45]

In a survey conducted by the *Financial Times* and Price Waterhouse in September 1996, BP was chosen by Europe's top executives as being one of the ten most respected European companies. The judges' criteria: "quality and implementation of corporate strategy, management of complexity, and skill at balancing the interests of customers, employees, and shareholders."[46] Obviously, Simon's and Browne's peers believe that BP is on the right track.

BP has weathered its sea changes admirably—the company's transformation as well as the transition from Simon's to Browne's leadership—but it may prove difficult in the future to keep employees as motivated as they were during the organization's restructuring. Browne is aware of this: "In order to be in control of your destiny, you must realize that you will stay ahead competitively only if you acknowledge that no advantage and no success is ever permanent. The winners are those who keep moving. We have tried to instill this attitude in our people."

During his tenure as CEO, Simon had the habit of closing meetings with a quote from Dickens. Shortly after taking on the CEO job at BP, Browne broke with his predecessor's tradition and ended a meeting with a quote from Shakespeare's *As You Like It:* "I will tell you the beginning; and if it pleases [you], you may see the end, for the best is yet to do."[47]

CHAPTER NINE

An Interview with David Simon and John Browne

David Simon does not leave you untouched. His warmth, charm, wit, incisiveness, energy, and genuine interest in people make those around him feel good. One's first impression is of an unpretentious individual who is given to understatement. This does not mean that he is laid back. On the contrary, there is an intensity and compulsion about him. One can imagine that—if the occasion warrants it—he can be a very hard-nosed businessman, a person with a strong drive to succeed whatever his objectives may be. If he believes in something, he really goes for it. But the striving part of him is easier to accept because of his playfulness. You are quickly won over by his charm and humor.

Simon is incisive, extremely thoughtful, very likable. He has a rare capacity to relate to people from different backgrounds. He is very empathic—an ability that helps him inspire people and get the best out of them. It enables him to pull people through difficult situations with minimum resistance.

It is a pleasure to see Simon operate at public functions. He is no wallflower at cocktail parties; he knows how to work the crowd and has a personal word for everyone. His excellent memory and instinctive sense of what makes people tick enable him to rise above the platitudes so common at such occasions. He understands the advantages of showing a genuine interest in all facets of the person he is talking to, and not limiting a conversation to work. Simon knows how to listen, and how to put others at ease. This is not just a superficial social skill. He has a genuine interest in people. It is something that comes to him naturally. People respond by opening up to him spontaneously and informatively.

Simon is the kind of reflective practitioner rarely found in business. He a businessman who not only acts but also reflects on the meaning and impact of his actions. He is extremely thoughtful. He is an emotional "sensor" who is gifted at picking up elusive signals. He is very good at assessing the dynamics of interpersonal and group situations. This makes him highly effective in such situations, and a skilled team player. He is also extremely well read. In that respect—in spite of his passion for sports—he is a true intellectual, interested in a wide range of subjects.

Simon is anything but dull. His verbal skills are considerable, helped by his command of several languages and great sense of humor. His political and business savvy serve him well in his new role as a cabinet minister, as they did while he was at BP.

John Browne makes a much more serious impression than David Simon. He is less playful, more controlled. He appears very achievement-oriented and extremely focused. Moreover, he has a strong vision of what BP should be like in the future; the vision also entails concerns about the social responsibility of an energy industry giant such as BP.

What do you like most about your job?

DAVID SIMON: It's never dull! Actually, the thing I like most about it is that I've never got out of bed in the morning not wanting to go to the office. *That's* a hell of a good test.

Is there anything about your job that causes sleepless nights?

SIMON: You do worry about the shocks and surprises. If you have a very good system and team, then fortunately you don't have to worry that much. But there are always the surprises. Environmental issues are always a big worry for anybody in our business. Nobody wants to be caught in an awful accident, a terrible oil spill, the tanker that goes astray. I think it's those unforeseen—really tragic—environmental events which cause you to lose sleep. If the team can't cope with that, there's not much you can do.

If you had known then what you know now, would you have taken on the job of CEO and later chairman?

SIMON: Oh yes. No question about that. The great thing about being in love with the business is that you can look at it from any angle, a new one, and find something interesting. The challenge of looking at it from a different perspective, I think, is extremely rewarding.

Part of the leadership role is generating that excitement for other people. You should know how to give the buzz to other people. It's part of what you're paid for. I would be very disappointed if, when people came to my room to chat about anything, they didn't go out feeling that this was an exciting business. They shouldn't go out thinking: "God almighty, not another bloody problem!"

What do you dislike most about your job? Many of the executives I talk to mention downsizing. Firing people is a very difficult thing to do.

SIMON: This is a difficult job. I don't want you to go away with the idea that because I get out of bed with enthusiasm to go to work, this is an easy thing to do. I think it is very demanding. I know there are going to be very difficult parts of my job, but I don't spend a lot of time trying to work out which are the most difficult.

You don't worry about "being the dentist"—inflicting some pain sometimes?

SIMON: That's what I'm paid for. That's what the shareholders expect the CEO to do, to get the business in shape for value growth over time.

What do you spend your time on?

SIMON: Talking. Listening. Persuading. It's a varied calendar. Two-way communication in all its aspects is the most vital part of the job.

What are some of the risky things you have done in your life?

SIMON: Being in the oil business is one big risk. Everyone thinks that because there are big numbers, this is a pretty easy business—you just pull the lever and the money comes out. If you knew the odds of a drill hole being successfully wet rather than dry, you would know a lot about the risks we take every day in this business. If it wasn't that way, you wouldn't enjoy the business.

Your career at BP has been very successful. Can you say something about the major decisions you've made at BP?

SIMON: I think all the major decisions involved new jobs within BP—I've moved more than ten times. In good companies, you are given a good choice of jobs. It was also a very important time for me when, after spending four years in the marketing division, I went to INSEAD to get an MBA. To take a year out and then come back into the company and continue your career is an act of faith. I can remember when I came back from INSEAD, I expected to go back to marketing because that's what I knew, and then suddenly the company said, "Why not switch over to logistics and computing?" Interesting decision at that stage.

Why was your INSEAD business school experience valuable?

SIMON: The most important thing for me technically was covering the issues that a liberal arts education in the UK does not give. Things to do with the numbers side of business—accountancy, statistics, quantitative analysis. Trying to fit together my experience in the soft cultures—people management, communication in every sense, speaking, and writing—with the numerate cultures. And then fitting that into a framework. That was one. Secondly, the cultural experience. The unbelievable advantage of spending a year in different cultural circumstances—language, understanding, beliefs, prejudices—and to get practice in getting all that out of the way before you get to solve business problems.

Has that been useful for you at BP?

SIMON: Absolutely vital, vital. We work in seventy markets around the world; I spent the first twenty years of my working career in covering ten different markets in Europe. Knowing some of the culture and the political background is half way, if not more than half way, to getting the solution, in my view.

Two things about culture: you have the corporate culture of BP, and of course you have the national culture. Originally, BP was based on a British culture. Is BP evolving and becoming less British?

SIMON: In a sense, it is a misconception that it is an English culture. It is an Anglo-Saxon culture more than English culture. There have been three phases in the cultural life of BP. The initial phase was the Middle East–British link. There was an English culture then, but the wealth of the company was created in the Gulf, and so most of the people who worked abroad worked in the Middle East. We had an international culture based on the Middle East for fifty years. Then in the late 1960s, the whole structure of the Gulf changed, and the oil companies lost their concessions, and BP had to reinvent itself. We reinvented ourselves as a U.S.-UK culture because when we found oil in Prudhoe Bay in Alaska, we became the biggest producer of oil in the United States. That led us to assimilate a U.S. culture. We then had a twenty-year period when the dominant cultural influence was American and European. Since the late 1980s, as our markets have shifted more to the east—southeast Asia, Eastern Europe, and China—we have moved beyond that strong Anglo-Saxon base.

Is this reflected in the membership of the board?

SIMON: Yes, it is. We currently have two Americans on the board, and have had for ten years. We have had Europeans, British, German, Irish, Scottish, and one Welshman—myself! So we have a European base. What we haven't yet done is to put an Eastern face on the board. It will happen, but it is much more difficult to manage logistically.

You have formed a dyad with John Browne. How does that work?

SIMON: I think the role of the chairman is to manage the board and to discuss with the chief executive what issues are relevant both in the day-to-day running of the company and on a longer-term basis. To guide and mentor the chief executive on behalf of the board on strategic issues and to be the ultimate link between the board as a team and the executive. To be the lubricant between those two systems. By and large, that's how we make the division; but since [he and I] have been in the business a long time and we are good friends, it really is a continuous conversation about the issues we are trying to develop strategically in the business. It is boundaryless.

We just talk about the business rather like we were talking about planning process. I suspect we are both in love with the business, and therefore we talk about it incessantly. Really, the complementarity at the first level is that a lot of my responsibilities involve looking outside, and a lot of John's primary responsibilities involve looking inside at the running and implementation. We complement each other in that way. We both look in and out in different ways, but when we have the conversation, it should be seamless and boundaryless.

How do you complement each other in other ways?

SIMON: (laughs) He can count, for a start. He's a seriously trained technologist and I'm a liberal arts person, so there's a difference, for a start.

BP in the past was characterized as very functional and hierarchical. Recently, it has been transformed to more of a networking type of organization. How did this happen?

SIMON: It happened initially because of liberalization of markets and the free flow of information. Pressure from the markets causes structural change in businesses. Because of the openness and liberalization of markets, our structure has had to change. That process brought about not only the splitting up of the company into separate profit units, but also cultural changes over the last twenty years: better understanding of how to run a business, better people within the business, and better use of information. So we like to think of ourselves as more of an asset-based organization. The people who run the assets can take decisions to make the assets work to the best advantage for the shareholders. They are the people who have the data every day about where the marketplace is; they take the best decisions. It is not the board who can take the decisions on how to run assets; that's not their job.

But the board can take some decisions on how to run the business. What I mean is, you paint a very deterministic picture—these are the markets that are changing and as result we had to act that way. But somebody had to translate those changes into some kind of plan of action for the company's future evolution.

SIMON: I think the board's role is setting that direction, I agree. The board decides things like what businesses should we be in, what are the balances between the businesses, how many assets should we have in a particular area. The board has to decide on the strategic background. But the board doesn't decide without the benefit of a dialogue with the people who are running the business down the line.

You are a strong advocate of targeting.

SIMON: I am a very strong advocate of hard targeting, benchmarking, and competition; knowing the targets for each of the assets of the business, in each of the businesses and in the group as a whole; knowing what your competition is, what they achieve, and what you have to achieve to do more than they. Everything in this business is potentially benchmarkable. Improvement should be continuous.

I remember an anecdote about the oil platform. . . .

SIMON: Yes. I ask: "How much money do you make?" An employee will reply: "I can tell you much oil we produce." I say: "Yes, but I am not interested in how much oil you produce; this is a factory for me. Where's the money?" Oil is only relevant in terms of money for the shareholders, not in terms of barrels. That's very important. It's part of the change that can be implied by the direction the board takes. The board can say: "We want this to be a performing culture; we want this culture to understand much more about the commercial than the technical merits of the business." Those are very deep-seated cultural issues.

But how did you do it? How do you change the mind-set of sixty thousand people?

SIMON: You spend a lot of time talking. And a lot of time listening. It's dialogue. The process of direction and planning and agreeing on targets and agreeing on allocation of resources in this business is a continuous dialogue. Planning, to us, is a living dialogue. I think it's important to have a very clear numerate focus—what is it we want to achieve? What are the targets related to change and the process of change? The whole organization can indulge in that dialogue on a continuous basis, but it is resolved, it is clear, it isn't just a messy discussion. At some point in time people will be able to say, "This is what we are going to do." Then people know why things are changing, and they can take pride in having achieved benchmarks along the way. That's how we do it.

How do you find out what's going on in your organization? There is always wariness in an organization, no matter how democratic or participative it may be. People tend to tell the leader what he wants to hear. How do you avoid that?

SIMON: It's mainly conversation. If you have been in a place for thirty-five years, you've got lots of contacts. This is a wandering-around type of place. This is a wandering-around type of building. All the directors live in a circle around this floor where we are sitting now. So you wander around and talk to people. The secretarial network is unbelievable in a culture like BP. You have to take time to talk to the secretaries, because they see life another way. There is a wonderful information system between the drivers. Anybody who believes their drivers don't know what's going on in their company doesn't understand the company. The people who bring you a cup of coffee: they'll tell you plenty. You should pass the time of day with people. It's not wishy-washy; it's double-checking what is an otherwise brilliant formal reporting system. I only have to read the books that people produce to know exactly where the numbers are. In a performance-based organization, you always have numbers. What you are asking me about is the soft data. What's the "sniff," as I call it, of the business? That's the drivers, tea ladies, the secretaries, the people you meet in the corridor. And as they always say, when you have a pee you should not waste time.

The change process was set in motion by your predecessor, Robert Horton, but somehow things went wrong. He left the boat, and you took over. You made it a very successful process. What did you do differently?

SIMON: First of all, every time we change the management system at BP in terms of the individuals, it is usually the signal for a change in style and approach. My predecessor, with the help of the people in his team—it's never down to one person in a big company— realized that, at the beginning of this process, behavioral change would be very important. We could not achieve the changes in the way we performed unless we changed the way we behaved as a company. We were rather a bureaucratic, stylized, functional model. We had to get out of that bureaucratic model. The question was, How to do it? We spent two years, from 1990 to 1992, more or less obsessed inside the company with cultural change, behavioral change, how to treat each other differently, what things we needed to do to respond to the changes in the outside environment.

What did I do specifically? All I did was to say the outcome of this change must be that certain targets are achieved. It was to take a behavioral process into a performance process. The only way you get things to perform, in my view, is to set targets and measure progress. If you don't measure it, you don't do it, we say in BP. Picking the right targets is a skill in itself.

The real change was focusing on how cultural change should really change performance in the company. I was bold enough to say, "These are the performance targets we have to hit"; to make the targets known to our shareholders; and to say, "This is what we are going to do." Funnily enough, that is quite an unusual process.

Your predecessor started that change process and got a fairly hostile reaction. But then you came into the picture and, although you took very dramatic action, people accepted it much more willingly. Why are you not known as Simon the Hatchet Man, for example?

SIMON: Because I never aspired to create that image for myself. I think in a company where you have a very strong culture, as we did, and you are changing, you have to have teams of people who are working. The process cannot be dependent on the will of one man. Leadership in a large institution, in my view, is nearly always about a group of people who have been able to build up a common vision and who then take the matter in groups and break it down. With sixty thousand people, the top six people in the company can, if they are lucky, touch fifty, the next fifty touching the next five hundred, and so it builds up. It is a continuous process of teams being built. The leadership must create a positive environment for this process. Leaders must behave like a team and perform themselves.

Teamwork is absolutely vital. When I took over—because I believe not only in targets but also in relatively easily communicable slogans—I had one slogan which was, "Performance, reputation, and team work." This was going to be the basis of the stylistic change that we were going to implement. If you ask the people, I think that the team I was leading was more focused, happier, and more united in what it was trying to achieve with the rest of the system. I can only perceive leadership in the context of the effectiveness and coherence of the top team. That's what the leader has to achieve. You judge the leader's individual capacity by the effectiveness of the team. That's what I call leadership.

How do you pick your key people? What do you look for?

SIMON: Integrity. Enthusiasm. Humor. I think humor is about putting things into perspective. It's about which mirrors you are shining on life, and how you view things. I think people who don't have humor don't understand perspective in every sense of the word. If people don't have perspective when they get to a level where they have big responsibility, they are potentially dangerous. I like people who are able to defray the pressure of decision and the pressure of conclusion by taking perspective. Humor is a good indicator of that capacity.

Obviously, integrity and enthusiasm and commitment are first because work is demanding, and you need these capacities to deliver. But having fun, the buzz, the humor is, in my view, what makes the difference between the organization being machinelike or a real part of life. I don't like the idea of business being shut off and serious and life being outside the office. If you can't make business as meaningful as life and a real part of life, I think you have the wrong perspective on it.

JOHN BROWNE: Mainly, we are looking for people who can work in teams. They have to be people who understand their strengths and limitations and how they fit, almost like a gene, with somebody else. They have to understand that.

You have said that you want to make BP a distinctive company. It is not clear what you mean by that.

BROWNE: It's very easy in business and industry to become a generic oil company, a generic grocery company. Companies imitate each other very quickly now. I think we at BP compete in distinctive ways. These are ways that endure and make us more strongly competitive. For example, we have distinctive assets. They are assets that other people can't own because there are few of them and we have a disproportionate share of them. In exploration and production, that's giant oil fields; so that's why we have been saying we have a very simple strategy—we go and find giant fields. Giant fields have tremendous advantages: low cost, they tend to have smaller fields attached to them geologically, and if you have more than someone else [does,] you can compete better. Same with market shares. I know it's old-fashioned to talk about having big market shares, but the fact is that if you have a large market share in a good market and you treat it well, few others can have that. Technology provides distinctiveness: intellectual know-how that nobody else has. For example, in our chemicals business we create materials that nobody else can create. That's something that allows us to build a competitive edge, a barrier.

The other elements of distinction are far away from these rather hard things I've talked about. First, our relationships with the world—customers, suppliers, governments, nongovernmental organizations, communities, and so on. We think of these as long-term and based on mutual advantage. And then organization, the process by which you motivate people, how you get motivation and creativity, and how you get people to learn from one another and share know-how.

But there is very often an inverse relation between size and creativity and innovation. You have sixty thousand employees throughout the world. So how do you do it?

BROWNE: We broke the business down into smaller business units to give people a sense of ownership. It's easier.

SIMON: The distinctiveness of the organization is for us: How do we create a buzz, meaning the attitude thing, the fun? So that we are not just another oil company.

BROWNE: Business is a deeply creative experience. People say: "Goodness me, an oil company; you are a predinosaur activity, one foot in the preindustrial revolution." And I say to them, "Wrong!" One measure of the creativity and modernity of any organization is to just look at the employment of engineers and scientists who solve physical problems. Solving physical problems requires creativity.

I talked earlier about the dramatic transformation of the organization from a functional, hierarchical company to a much more networking kind of organization. That was not an easy task, particularly for such a large organization as this one.

BROWNE: Process became an important part of BP and indeed is the heart of the organization design now. The second thing that happened was that people began to say there is too much complexity. The chances are that if you take a lot of it away, you will still get the same result and maybe even get a better result because people will be freer. Today, for example, we still have the complexities of the world, but we think of the complexities being managed by process, not by organizational structure. The ultimate catalyst was a lot of investment in behavior.

SIMON: Seminars, discussions, role playing.

BROWNE: The very embryonic ideas on process, the multiple experimentation, the understanding of behavior began to shape the organization that has developed, and developed and developed. Now we have an organization which is really distinctively flat. Very flat indeed. That wasn't the purpose, but it was the outcome. BP is now divided into business units, linked by process, deeply committed to learning, deeply committed to motivation, and working on getting more creativity in the organization.

Actually, when you talk about people who are creative with a capital C, it's usually the lonely explorers.

BROWNE: I think we are looking for a different form of creativity. We are looking for creativity that allows people to have good ideas. If you have enough people with initiative, I think you have an organization that is creative. It's the bit you can't see. You can say we have great assets, great organizations, great people, great technology . . . and you can say, "Well, so what?" When you have people who can operate in this way, thinking about how they affect others and how it works as a whole—and if leadership is very clear on the direction, on the boundaries, giving support and encouragement to people—then I think you have got something which in a "magical" way—and this a strategic word—does something different.

Do you feel the employment contract has been changed?

BROWNE: Of course it has, but it has been changed from one that wasn't written to another one that still isn't written. People understand that, but it may make them feel insecure in certain ways.

A certain amount of discomfort can be a good thing.

BROWNE: You have to have a balance, but you have be very human about it. If you have too much insecurity, you have a subsistence existence where people cannot be creative; they won't take risks.

Did many people leave in the process of behavior change?

BROWNE: Yes. It's tough to say how many left involuntarily [and how many] voluntarily. We spent several years with one mission—cost cutting—and that's very painful.

SIMON: As we moved out of the initial stages of the change process—from behavior change and discussion about behavior change, and discussion about openness and communicating better—into performance, I thought the targeting process and overt commitment of the top of the company to achieving certain hard targets was very important. In a sense, I learned some of that from your side of the business, John. Do you think that was important in the culture as a whole?

BROWNE: Absolutely crucial. It's now to the point where, if we defined our core values, setting targets would be one of them. And it has positive and negative aspects. This company believes it's in the business of making promises and delivering them. It's a deeply held belief. That's the good news—very, very good news. The bad news is, of course, people have to worry about what promises are made. It's a very tough balance, getting the right promises—targets—made, both quantitative and nonquantitative, and motivating our people.

When I talk about how we compete, we talk in little phrases—but they're important phrases. We talked about assets, organization, technology. The fourth is relationships, because in this industry in particular, what counts is the equality of the relationships that you build. This allows you to build business, create opportunities, and also create a sense that you are doing something worthwhile because you are doing something for somebody else.

Percy Barnevik of ABB has said that you cannot really motivate employees by return on investment and profit maximization. You have to do something more. He stresses pragmatic idealism while being competitive, doing something for society while making money. Do you think about those issues?

BROWNE: Employees have to go home and feel good about this. They have to withstand the criticism that may come from children and neighbors. Are you doing something that is worthwhile, or are you a necessary evil? The confidence that we are doing something that is really worthwhile, and then doing it successfully, is the thing that will attract good people to us and will keep the good people with us, and will keep people thinking about the future.

SIMON: I would say a strong distinguishing feature of the company over time—certainly the company that I joined thirty-five years ago—is service. There is a strong integrity inside the group to try and do something which is good. One of the problems that our generation found was that it was doing something that was good but that didn't necessarily make money. You had to change that feeling that the company was a good company, it had integrity, it understood service, it understood how to handle communities, in a very measured and sensible way. But the trouble was it didn't necessarily know how it made money. That's the balance that we have had to bring to the organization.

Where is BP headed?

SIMON: I think it's headed down a path of differentiation, in performance terms. It's going to be a very different type of organization from the one I grew up with. I think it will be distinctive in its sector of the industry, and will give everybody a great deal of pleasure.

How would you like to be remembered? I know you are a team player, but what kind of things are important to you?

SIMON: That's a serious sort of question, and you know me, I'm unlikely to give a serious answer. I think one of the nicest epitaphs I've heard for anybody is: "That's a guy I'd like to go and have a drink with." I think that's a nice epitaph.

KEY POINTS

BP's Unique Competitive Edge:

Creating a distinctive organization (distinctive assets, technology, and relationships with the outside world; and the process by which the company fosters creativity, learning, and the sharing of knowledge)

- Corporate culture
  - Accountability.
  - Values that are inviolate: ethics, health, safety, and the environment.
  - Simple goals, use of acronyms.
  - "Targeting is fundamental to achieving."
  - Sharing of experience and best practice throughout all levels.
  - "Performance, reputation, and teamwork."
- Leadership style
  - Emotional intelligence: able to empathize with and channel subordinates' emotions.
  - Accessible group leader: engenders honest, focused, and persuasive communication.
  - Personal contact at all levels.
  - Well-balanced leadership dyad.
  - Pragmatic idealism: provide energy in a safe and careful way.
  - Leader as team player.
  - Generate excitement at all levels.
- Organizational design
  - Decision making pushed down to local levels.
  - Small business units.
  - Very flat, team-based organization.
  - Build on strengths rather than through diversification.
- Continuous transformation and change
  - Recognize that it is a sequential emotional process.
  - Learning is key to adapting in rapidly changing environments.
  - Decentralizing encourages personal initiative and creativity.
  - "Change for change's sake is not on the agenda."

- "Improvement should be continuous."
- "People should know why things are changing."
• Building a global organization
  - Leader (Simon) is more European than British, thanks to family background, early work experience, and a gift for languages.
  - Decision making at local levels.
  - Mixed-nationality executive board.

Conclusion: Practices of Vanguard Companies

Dealing with the ambiguities that the new change-oriented, boundaryless organization creates is a major challenge—one that leaders clinging to past ways are not equal to. Many organizational leaders, trained in a bureaucracy that is no longer relevant, are deficient in nurturing the creative potential of their people. They do not know how to create the kind of learning culture that transforms itself rather than being changed and manipulated by outside forces; as a result, their organizations and their people are reactive rather than proactive. They fail to create new leadership in their organizations, and they fail to develop their people. Furthermore, they fail to provide the material rewards and symbolic actions that would earn the loyalty of their employees.

Even though executives of this ilk are at the helm of organizations the world over, they are leaders in name only. Effective leaders—like Branson, Simon, and Barnevik—believe that if people are given the opportunity to spread their wings, they may really take off. More important, true leaders believe that such flight is the ultimate goal. They know that competitive advantage based on the knowledge, creativity, and goodwill of their people is hard to duplicate.

In their roles as charismatic leaders and architects, they have designed globally effective structures and strategies, fostered a corporate culture that glues together loosely organized units, and motivated their people to carry out the vision despite the emerging discontinuities in their environment. How can we encourage development of these strengths in ourselves and in our organizations? Answers can be found in the best practices and values that these three men espouse. In this concluding chapter, we look first at the best practices by expanding on the key points found at the end of each case. Then we turn to the meta-values underlying the corporate culture in these organizations that respond to people's need for identity and meaning in the workplace.

LEADERSHIP BEST PRACTICES

Probably the most important factor that makes these leaders and their organizations so successful is their clear vision of what they want to do and where they want to go. Because of the relentlessness with which they transmit their vision to their people, they create a sense of purpose within the organization. Vision is essential, as we saw earlier; it provides a road map for the future, generates excitement, creates order out of chaos, and offers criteria for success. But it is worthless if it is not shared by all the members of an organization.

Expressing the Vision. Branson, Barnevik, and Simon all have something of the showman in them. Branson's style is almost exhibitionist, Barnevik's style is a sophisticated mix of the rational and humanistic, and Simon's style is low-key and friendly. Although these leaders differ in style, all three have kept their vision simple. They exude enthusiasm and self-confidence when talking about what they hope to do and where they want to go, and this makes their vision contagious.

The Leader as Teddy Bear. All three of these men understand that their people are likely to feel a certain amount of discomfort as they are asked to go through discontinuous change. This is not all bad. Without a certain degree of discomfort, people may fall asleep. But there are clear limits how far one can go. These are people who possess empathy. Each man has a kind of teddy bear quality, an ability to recognize and contain followers' anxieties. Richard Branson has a real warmth and approachability, and he constantly encourages his employees to contact him directly with ideas or problems. David Simon combines his friendly emphasis on teamwork and equality with his insistence on measurement and targeting, effectively using soft people skills to build a foundation for hard results. Percy Barnevik has more of a left-brained, reserved character, but he has made walking the talk a high priority through his continuous contact with employees around the world.

Gaining Power by Sharing Power. Enthusiasm for a leader's vision never develops if it is rammed down followers' throats. These people know how to create a compelling, connecting vision. These CEOs realize that one does not lead by hoarding power. On the contrary, the CEO who pushes power down the line benefits in the long run. Although letting go of power may seem difficult or even chaotic in the short run (after all, power and control have an addictive quality), eventually the whole organization benefits. These people share information; they minimize secrecy; they get their people involved. Employees who feel they are making a difference become more productive. As a result of the organization's productivity, the CEO becomes more powerful. Branson, Barnevik, and Simon have avoided the trap that many other executives step into: allowing short-term psychological pleasure to overrule long-term tangible benefits. These CEOs know how to postpone the gratification of their more immediate power needs.

Choosing Complementary Colleagues. As a corollary to sharing power, by understanding their own inner theater these three leaders find people with strengths that compensate for their own weaknesses. Branson has had a series of strong executives. His first partner, Nik Powell, was methodical and cautious. He took on difficult tasks such as cost cutting and staff reduction. Simon Draper, "Mr. Golden Ears" at Virgin Music, forged Virgin's creative direction. Branson's brother-in-law, Robert Devereux, has a hands-off relationship with his boss, which gives him the freedom to bring Branson down to earth when necessary.

Barnevik depends on a number of colleagues who have been working with him for a long time, some giving him advice on long-term business developments, others giving him tactical support.

Simon, as CEO and later chairman, worked closely with John Browne. This genuine respect and interest in outside opinion has helped these CEOs to design realistic structures and strategies for their organizations.

STRUCTURE

Every organization attempting to create an exciting working environment faces the same dilemma: economies of scale are not without serious diseconomies of size. Larger size means more possibilities (for employees and the organization alike), but growth can easily lead to gridlock (as BP in particular discovered). Branson, Barnevik, and Simon know that when organizational units become too big, employees are inclined to become less involved.

Believing That Small Is Beautiful. To challenge their employees and to add to a sense of ownership, the three have minimized the negative aspects of corporate mass by embracing the concept that small is beautiful. They have gone to great lengths to create in their large corporations a small-business, familylike atmosphere in a high-performance workplace. "Tall" structures are out, and flat structures are in, encouraging lateral rather than vertical communication. Decentralization and operational autonomy are *sine qua non* for the creative and high-performance atmosphere found in Virgin, ABB, and BP. These organizations are of the kind where people experience a sense of personal growth.

Percy Barnevik's aim was for ABB to be both centralized and decentralized, big and small, global and local. Consequently, he created a company made up of five thousand profit centers. Richard Branson, working toward a similar big-small goal, spins a new business off an existing one as soon as there are more than fifty people working for it. Branson applies his philosophy religiously: his organization, like ABB, consists of a number of small, autonomous units run by self-managed teams.

Developing a Network Structure. Another significant way in which these successful CEOs maintain adaptability is through the network structure that underlies each organization's decision-making process. The loose organizational architecture of the three organizations is very similar. ABB and BP have a sophisticated global matrix structure with enormous fluidity between business-area managers and country managers. Virgin resembles a *keiretsu* organization of loosely linked companies in which employees have the constant opportunity to rewrite their job descriptions, depending on what new challenges they are prepared to undertake.

Abolishing Bureaucracy. In the new type of organizational structure favored by Branson, Barnevik, and Simon, large head offices— once needed to exert control over the operating companies—are no longer required. These executives have taken to heart the comments of the wit who once said that there is an inverse relationship between size of the head office and the success of an organization. After all, when there are too many people in head office, there are also too many people prepared to "help" the people running the operating units.

Branson does not have a head office, per se; he works from home. When he *did* have a head office, he worked from a houseboat—not a place that one can crowd with people. Barnevik's aversion for large head offices is well known. According to ABB's policy bible, an important guideline for acquiring companies is what it calls "the 30 percent rule." (Recall from Chapter Five that in newly acquired companies, personnel are cut dramatically—30 percent through eliminating some functions, another 30 percent through decentralizing certain functions into profit centers, and yet another 30 percent through creating service centers that invoice services at market rates. Applying the 30 percent rule means that only 10 percent of the staff remains.) Putting this rule in action, Barnevik created an ABB head office staffed by a mere 150 people, whereas before the merger Brown Boveri had four thousand people in Baden, Switzerland, and ASEA had two thousand people in Västerås, Sweden. During BP's transformation process, headquarters staff was likewise reduced—in its case from 3,000 to 380 people.

In all three organizations, *bureaucracy* is a dirty word. Executives at Virgin and ABB use a minimum amount of paper, preferring to use the telephone or fly around and see people in person. David Simon, when at BP, set a relatively informal tone at the helm with his relaxed manner and passion for sport. He always had a sporting metaphor ready to describe just about any action or event at BP.

The principle behind the nonbureaucratic organizational design favored by Branson, Barnevik, and Simon (and now

Browne) is that if people have a sense of control, they feel better about what they are doing; they are more creative, they feel that they are learning new things, and they show fewer symptoms of stress. Furthermore, if people feel a sense of ownership for a particular part of the organization, they are more committed.

Achieving the Flat Organization. Branson, Barnevik, and Simon believe that one of the most important factors in keeping the momentum going is encouraging creative energy at *all levels* of the organization. As organizational architects, they designed (or redesigned) their corporate culture to inspire people wherever they happen to be positioned in the organization. In addition, they foster a sense of ownership in their people, building a strong foundation for loyalty. They believe strongly that strategic awareness should not be limited to the top echelons of the organization but should be pushed deep down. Barnevik, for example, has pushed authority, responsibility, and accountability so far down into the organization at ABB that now there are never more than five people between the CEO and the shop floor. At BP, business units work directly with the nine-member executive group. The lack of hierarchy at Virgin is proverbial: the company is as flat as any organization could be. All three organizations are not only flat but simple, to minimize the potential for confusion in the decision chain. The success of these companies suggests that organizational structure can actually constitute a competitive advantage.

STRATEGY

The structures Branson, Barnevik, and Simon have put in place—with the added advantage of sophisticated information systems—help their organizations be as flexible and customer-oriented as many smaller companies.

Staying on Top of Technology. Designing an organization of the type we have described would have been impossible until recently. Being big and small at the same time, functioning as a number of small, loosely connected companies, yet maintaining the organization's cohesiveness—this approach is feasible only because of the revolution in information technology. Information systems such as

BP's global virtual team network or ABB's ABACUS system have become a major force pulling geographically dispersed employees together. It is now possible for top executives in any organization to decentralize without losing a sense of control, and for employees to work with colleagues on the other side of the world. Naturally, success in these new structures requires literacy in modern information and communication technology.

Appearances may deceive: even Virgin, with its apparently loose structure, has a centralized data-processing unit to monitor the information flow. Information technology has made it possible for Virgin to evolve like an amoeba, continuously dividing and reproducing. Virgin is presently a subtle network of interrelated companies with a mutuality of interests—which notion can be mystifying to outsiders. To some extent, Branson's company is a virtual organization. Information technology is crucial at BP as well. One of the benefits of decentralization and improved information technology at BP has been an increase in personal initiative and breakthrough thinking.

Focusing on the Customer. Another critical theme in the design of these organizations is customer orientation. Close customer contact for everyone in the company is a major part of the business philosophy espoused by Branson, Barnevik, and Simon, and superior customer satisfaction colors the design of their organizational processes. The process starts at the top. All three executives are known for their focus on the customer. Close customer contact increases the employees' sense of ownership and encourages them to feel responsible for maintaining customers' interest and goodwill. In these organizations, a process orientation—how best to help the customer—is preferred over a functional structure. Customers are neither abstractions nor distractions. Again, the small-business-within-a-large-corporation style of these three organizations enhances the possibility of contact and improves the feedback loop. Barnevik accounts for his company's performance in terms of size: "Our strategy of delegating responsibility to many small profit centers is a winning one. It puts our people close to customers and lets them see how their decisions and attention to customer needs contribute to ABB's growth. This, in turn, frees up rich human resources of initiative and energy. We want to achieve management by motivation and goals instead of by instruction and directives. . . . Adopt the right priorities: Customer first, ABB Group second, own profit center third."[1]

Reducing Response Time. Branson, Barnevik, and Simon all emphasize the importance of speed—particularly Simon at BP, which is a firm once considered to be about as wieldy and rapid as its own supertankers. Product life cycles are growing ever shorter, and speed-to-market has become increasingly important. Too many companies have invented great products only to lose out in the process of market introduction.

Branson, Barnevik, and Simon have created dynamic, fast-paced environments in which employees are constantly challenged and can expect quick action and results. Simon's first move when he became CEO was to set up a three-part target for turning the company around—a target that was attained within two years. One of the key success factors in Branson's organization has likewise been the ability to act fast: "I can have an idea in the morning in the bathtub," he once said, "and have it implemented in the evening."[2] Speed also has an essential place in Barnevik's management philosophy. In his policy bible, he says that "it is better to be roughly right with respect to speed." He makes it very clear that it is permissible to make mistakes that are due to speed. Indeed, failing to take action and losing opportunities because of reluctance to make decisions is the only unacceptable behavior at ABB.

CORPORATE CULTURE

What holds the dynamic but diverse groups of people together in a sprawling global organization? There are two kinds of glue at work in loosely structured organizations. We have already mentioned one kind: sophisticated information systems. The other kind is shared values. What *attracts* dynamic people to these organizations? Branson, Barnevik, and Simon have made it clear that their people are challenged and rewarded according to their contributions. How do these leaders prepare their people for discontinuity? They expect them to feel responsible for the future of the organization, and encourage learning, initiative, and—perhaps most important—adaptability.

Fostering Shared Values. These three CEOs encourage (implicitly or explicitly) each organizational participant to share certain values specific to their respective corporation—values that go beyond their national culture—and this management strategy stimulates cohesiveness. At ABB, the key values are summarized in the policy bible. At Virgin, they are more subtly instilled. At BP, they are grafted on to the company's deep expertise in technology. But everyone at all three organizations is expected to be familiar with the corporate culture of the organization. New recruits are indoctrinated in these values, which are reaffirmed in workshops, seminars, and meetings. People are expected to internalize the corporate values and behave accordingly, with a positive payoff: internalization of corporate values means less need for external controls. Most important, however, companies tend to perform better if their employees have shared values.

Instilling Good Corporate Citizenship. Branson, Barnevik, and Simon attempt to make good corporate-citizen behavior—that is, setting organizational goals above one's personal agenda—an essential part of their value system. One of the things that make their companies so successful is that employees are prepared to go out of their way to help each other and preserve the integrity of the organization. In contrast to what is found in many other organizations, their employees do not take a parochial attitude to their jobs. They are always prepared to go beyond the particular job requirements. What is important to them is the greater good of the organization. But good citizenship does not just happen in the workplace; leaders have to set the tone. Barnevik reminds his executives of the need to walk the talk. The top executives of Virgin are always ready to give a helping hand where needed. Simon's style was to encourage people to see him as part of the team.

Cultivating Open Communication. Although shared corporate values are important, Branson, Barnevik, and Simon make a great effort to create the sort of environment in which contrarian thinking is tolerated. They have taken to heart General Patton's comment that "when everyone agrees, somebody is not thinking." They realize that if people do not have the confidence to say what they mean, the CEO receives filtered information. Barnevik acknowledges the potential risk of not getting enough feedback and works to ensure full communication. Simon is known as a good communicator who tries to "listen first, think next, and act after."[3] Branson has an open-door policy. In some ways, he is the ombudsman of his organization. He welcomes critical comments about how to improve the operation of his companies and is always prepared to listen (and, crucially, to act) when people have legitimate complaints. These three leaders do not kill the bearer of bad news. On the contrary, they handle negative communications constructively. And they set an example of openness; they make an enormous effort to practice what they preach. They take their role as coach, cheerleader, and mentor very seriously.

Offering Challenge and Expecting Success. Virgin, ABB, and BP attract employees who like exciting, immediate challenge. Senior executives in these organizations are willing to take a gamble on their challenge-hungry people, giving them permission to make mistakes. This does not mean, however, that employees are not held accountable for their performance. People are expected to take responsibility for their actions. Barnevik reminds people that delegation is not abdication.

It is impossible to be a winning institution anywhere—or to be a successful part of such an institution—without making a distinction between excellent and mediocre work. Thus constructive feedback about performance is crucial to the culture of these three organizations. They have compassion, but there is also a limit on excuses.

Rewarding Excellence. These three executives also realize that fostering top performers' loyalty to the organization is essential. This is more easily said than done, however, especially now that people expect tangible rewards rather than the old one-size-fits-all promise of lifetime employment. Imaginative human resource management systems have been put in place at Virgin, ABB, and BP to keep valued employees committed to the organization. Through effective reward systems, employees have come to expect reward according to contribution. Gainsharing—providing a piece of the action in the form of stock options, bonuses, or some other profit-sharing plan—is a way of tying high performers to an organization. Branson has said that he is in the business of making millionaires. He makes it quite clear that he does not want his high performers to leave Virgin to start their own companies elsewhere; he avoids this by allowing them the possibility of becoming millionaires under the Virgin umbrella. The various gainsharing vehicles also motivate people to reach peak performance. In late 1997, for example, ABB announced a new stock option program for its senior managers in a bid to focus managers' minds on shareholder returns. Top BP executives are given bonuses based on the company's performance over five years.

Successful leaders create an atmosphere that celebrates successes in less tangible ways as well. Small symbolic actions (such as taking a contract-winning team out for dinner, or staging awards for exceptional performers) go a long way toward motivating employees.

Building Commitment and Autonomy. During the transformation processes at BP and ABB, and on a continuing basis in Virgin, these three CEOs have gone to great lengths to facilitate the process of individual change, trying to bring on board those people who were merely going through the motions. As Barnevik observed:

> Take one of the 600 middle-level managers in Germany. He may be 50 years old and have worked in a stable environment for the past 25. He may have to work some extra hours, change his methods, perhaps switch to another job within the company, and he asks why the hell should he. You tell him it is to increase low profitability. He says we have had a nice life on a 2 percent margin for the past 25 years, so why do you want 5 percent or even 7 percent? Well, you talk of job security, long-term expansion, the threat from the [European] Community's single market, and that a strong company is good for him and his family. Somebody has got to talk to this man and motivate him to change, otherwise he'll just carry on the same way.[4]

These CEOs have learned through experience that changing individuals is hard, sometimes impossible. They know that a corporate culture that encourages employees to feel responsible for the future of the organization (and their own career) is much more effective at change than a culture that centralizes responsibility in its leaders. Abandoning the traditional command-and-control style of management and organization, which was designed for unskilled employees who counted on lifetime employment in exchange for loyalty—the broken psychological contract—they believe that the future of the high-performance organization lies in self-managed teams run by people with initiative. They try to attract people who set high standards for themselves, who criticize themselves when they fail to live up to those standards, and who feel intrinsically rewarded when they meet them.

Innovation and Learning. Branson, Barnevik, and Simon look for individuals who are eager to learn, understand how to adapt, are inner-driven, know how to manage their own career, and have a high tolerance for ambiguity. They know that bottlenecks in the flow of ideas often originate at the *top* of the organization. These leaders have created a continuous-learning culture, and in return they expect and look for ideas to come from people at all levels of their organizations.

Cultivating Harmony in a Global Organization. A useful metaphor for the kind of workplace that Branson, Barnevik, and Simon have created is that of a jazz combo, in which all the musicians work together to create harmonious music. Barnevik in particular has built a genuinely global organization in that ABB has no single national identity, and many "musicians" from different countries. The globalization of ABB's culture is both top-down (ABB's board is composed of a mix of executives from different nationalities) and bottom-up (young executives are continuously moved around to develop global experience). Simon and Browne's virtual team network allows their people to transfer learning from one part of the company to another regardless of geographical locations. Branson has tuned his people to look for opportunities wherever they may arise in the world.

For each player in these organizations, however, there is ample room to improvise as a soloist. These three leaders have focused on *process*: constructing the kind of high-performance learning organization that encourages individual contribution. They put a high value on their roles as guardian of culture and teacher. As

Barnevik has said, "Ninety percent of leadership is process; only 10 percent is strategy. Of that 10 percent, 2 percent is analysis and 8 percent is having the guts to make tough decisions."

META-VALUES FOR THE INFORMATION AGE

Although the best practices that we describe above go a long way toward explaining the success of many high-performance firms, they do not on their own provide a complete answer to the dilemmas facing global leaders. Given humankind's search for meaning and identity, and employees' sense of frustration over the breaking of the old psychological contract, what can we do to make life in organizations more rewarding?

When people are asked to describe the best work experience they have had, or to analyze the circumstances under which they felt most creative, useful, and productive, the response usually touches on one or more of these factors:

- Being involved in a startup activity
- Being involved in a turnaround activity
- Being part of a high-performance team
- Being engaged in successful mentoring

When we take a closer look at these reactions, we discover that they dovetail with the basic motivational systems—systems based on identity and meaning—described in the preface of this book.

This tells us that the best companies possess a set of meta-values that closely respond to the motivational needs described earlier. Richard Branson, Percy Barnevik, and David Simon have created high-performance organizations in which employees feel part of a community, enjoy what they are doing, and believe that they are contributing something to the world (believe that what they are doing *individually* makes a difference). These themes of "love," "fun," and "meaning" could be considered the underlying meta-values to be found in high-performance organizations.

Love. Since attachment and affiliation make for a powerful underlying motive in humankind's search for meaning, the first important meta-value contributing to exceptional performance is love.

In the framework of understanding the high-performance organization, the term implies creating a family feeling in the workplace, a sense of community. Why is this so important? There are several reasons, all interrelated. Attachment and affiliation are the basis for trust and mutual respect. A trusting culture in turn facilitates a learning culture, one where people are permitted to make mistakes and learn from them and are encouraged to compare their performance with that of companies considered to be the best in their fields. This blend of trusting and learning results in "distributed leadership"—leadership that is spread throughout the organization, shared among leaders and followers alike.

Organizations low on love—on the facilitating factor that produces trust and mutual respect—become dysfunctional.[5] Paranoid thinking takes hold in such organizations, along with existential loneliness (a basic form of anxiety), and people waste energy on defensive routines and ritualistic behavior rather than concentrating on teamwork and striving for excellence. (This was exactly the situation that arose at BP during its first, unsuccessful, restructuring program.) To avoid this kind of downward spiral, good corporate citizenship behavior—people's willingness to trust and help each other—should be strongly encouraged.

Branson, Barnevik, and Simon are acutely aware of the importance of trust as a corporate value and have made it a high priority. Communication, competence, credibility, consistency, support, respect, and honesty are key parts of the trust equation. All the leaders we have studied here are capable of taking both the good and the bad in their stride. They know the value of being consistent, they understand the need to support and respect their people, they recognize the importance of being honest, and they respond to the need for openness and communication. They make an enormous effort to listen to their people and to practice what they preach.

If this feeling of "love" is present, if the members of an organization have a real sense of community, they can do exceptional things. Among these three leaders, Richard Branson has probably gone the furthest to create such a feeling among his employees. But Barnevik and Simon have also made great efforts to foster a sense of community among their people.

In their roles of coach and cheerleader, Branson, Barnevik, and Simon are aware of the importance of generativity: helping their younger executives grow and develop, and taking vicarious pleasure in that process. Through this generativity, which allows their efforts to be continued through the work of successors, they create feelings of continuity and meaning. An appreciation of generativity contributed to smooth transitions at BP and ABB as Simon and Barnevik moved on to other things. Although Branson is strongly identified with his organization, he has developed a decentralized structure, and his *keiretsu*-like group of companies could probably carry on without him.

Fun. In these more effective companies, employees seem to enjoy themselves. If fun is a meta-value in an organization, the distinction between work and play disappears. Excellent companies, acutely aware of the link between play and creativity, encourage the playful potential of their people. The leaders of these companies recognize that if people have fun, they not only work harder but are also more creative and innovative. These leaders know that companies fostering creativity and innovation are winners in the global-competitive game.

Unfortunately, in too many companies fun is completely discounted as a value; those organizations resemble a kind of gulag. This makes the organizational experience an extremely heavy one. In organizations that fail to value fun, work is merely a chore, carried out with very little pleasure. Indeed, pleasure is seen as something permitted only outside the organization. Being in the workplace is like being locked up in a psychic prison. Employees behave like sleepwalking zombies, going through the motions without being fully present. With all enthusiasm pressed out of these people by the corporate culture, they lead depersonalized lives in depersonalized organizations.

But corporate life need not be so dismal. Insightful executives in high-performance organizations, of whom Richard Branson is a prime example, realize that turning work into an exciting adventure can make all the difference to employee attitudes and productivity. Branson said of Virgin, "We've done things differently, and that's made life more fun and enjoyable than if we'd taken a slightly more conservative approach. I've been determined to have a good time."[6]

Meaning. If what people do on the job is placed in the context of transcending one's own personal needs (as examples, improving the quality of life, helping people, or contributing to society)—in other words, if the meta-value of meaning is honored—the impact can be extremely powerful. Naturally, companies operating in certain industries have a competitive advantage. Consider the pharmaceutical industry, for instance. Being part of a group of people who are striving to preserve and improve human life through developing new medicines helps sustain the meta-value of meaning.

Branson, Barnevik, and Simon all make it clear that they want their people to feel proud of their organizations; they want them to experience their companies as something special. Barnevik says that he is motivated by a desire to make a better world by creating employment (particularly in Eastern Europe, where he is the largest investor), and to make the world more livable by providing clean energy and transportation. For Branson, too, social concerns are an important part of corporate philosophy. On many occasions, he has put his money where his mouth is. Just two instances of this are Virgin's producing low-priced Mates condoms in response to the AIDS crisis, and Branson's bidding for the national lottery franchise in the UK with a promise to donate all profits to charity. For British Petroleum, environmental issues are critically important. Some environmentalists concede that BP is at the forefront of multinational organizations taking global warming seriously. John Browne has said that environmental protection is a significant corporate cultural value: "We have an action plan in which 50,000 people [BP employees] participate."[7] As he said in a speech to the Royal Society in London, "Our employees have hopes for the world and for their children. . . ."

Engaging in a startup or turnaround activity also fosters a sense of meaning, as we noted earlier. This type of endeavor gratifies people's sense of exploration, allows them the opportunity to grow by doing something new, gives them a sense of community, and permits them to assert themselves. Creating something, which is the essence of startup work, also lets people feel that they are leaving some kind of legacy—the generativity that we spoke of earlier.

The antidote to humankind's fear of death is to create meaning. The challenge for organizational leaders is to recognize the need for meaning and create circumstances that allow people in organizations to go beyond narrowly defined organizational vision and mission statements. Organizational leaders have the responsibility to institute collective systems of meaning. They have to create conditions that reveal a congruence between personal and collective objectives so that the work done in their organizations makes sense to the people doing it. This congruence comes about only if employees' motivational need systems are aligned with organizational values that allow people to make their subjective experiences and actions meaningful.

There is rich interplay among all of the meta-values found in high-performance organizations. As part of the quest for meaning, organizational leadership must encourage a sense of community and continuity in the organization, allow people to play (in its broadest sense), give people the opportunity to express themselves creatively and fully, and highlight the worth of organizational tasks. Employees should enjoy the conviction that they are appreciated as individuals, that their contributions make a difference. Such congruence between the inner and outer worlds promotes both individual and organizational health; it lays the groundwork for a new psychological contract in organizations.

A SUMMING UP

It is clear from the examples of these three leaders that autocratic leadership has no place in the organization of the future. As Dwight Eisenhower said, "You don't lead people by hitting them over the head; that's assault, not leadership." Organizations are looking for authoritative leaders, people who inspire confidence and command respect and loyalty because they demonstrably know what they are talking about and act on their beliefs.

Richard Branson, Percy Barnevik, and Sir David Simon are excellent models of authoritative leadership, outstanding practitioners of the charismatic and architectural roles. Unlike many organizational leaders, they are aware of the quirks of their own inner theater; they have built on their individual strengths and mitigated their weaknesses to the advantage of their organizations.

Furthermore, they are sensitive to the complexities of thought and action in those around them. Realizing that they cannot do things alone, they tap the creativity of everybody in their organizations. They make employment an exciting, meaningful journey—and in so doing create world-class companies.

These leaders have really made a difference. Through their example, others may be inspired to do the same, developing their organizations (and the individuals in them) to their fullest potential.

Notes

Introduction

1. Johansson, G. "Percy Barnevik's Recipe for Growth That Has Something for Everyone." *Dagens Industri/Europa,* Feb. 4, 1994, pp. 10–11.
2. Kennedy, C. "ABB: Model Merger for the New Europe." *Long Range Planning,* 1992, *25*(5), 14.

PART ONE: RICHARD BRANSON

Chapter One

1. "Republican Hot Air." (Editorial.) *Daily Telegraph,* Jan. 8, 1997.

Chapter Two

1. The bulk of this case is based on interviews by Manfred Kets de Vries and the case writer, Robert Dick, with Richard Branson, Robert Devereux, Trevor Abbott, Simon Draper, Don Cruickshank, Will Whitehorn, and other key executives of Virgin. An interview was also conducted with Branson's parents. Background material for this chapter was taken from the following sources: "Virgin Atlantic, Still on Course." *Economist,* Jan. 22, 1994, p. 61; "Virgin Group Plans Stock Buy-Back," *International Herald Tribune,* October 5, 1988, p. 13; Bowditch, G. "Entrepreneur Too Old to Play the Foolish Virgin." *Times,* Apr. 6, 1991, p. 23; Branson, R. "Growing Bigger While Staying Small." Director-Annual Convention Special, 1995, pp. 60–68; Branson, R. Speech to the Institute of Directors, 1993; Brown, M. Richard Branson. London: Michael Joseph, 1988; Burger, W. "Up, Up, and Away: Peter Pan's Empire." *Newsweek,* June 13,

1994, pp. 28–33; Campsie, J. "A Fresh Approach." *Marie-Claire*, Nov. 1997, p. 338; Cochrane, A. "How the Hell Does Branson Manage It?" *Management Weekly*, July 1991, pp. 47–51, 114–116; Coleman, B., and Hudson, R. "British Air to Pay Damages to Virgin Atlantic for Libel." *Wall Street Journal Europe*, Jan. 13, 1993, p. 3; Davidson, A. "Virgin Plots New Route into Media." *Sunday Times*, Oct. 14, 1990, p. 11; Gregory, M. "Dirty Tricks: The Story of British Airways' Secret War Against Virgin Atlantic." *Sunday Times*, Mar. 13, 1994, sect. 4, pp. 1–3; Ipsen, E. "Thorn to Buy Virgin for £510 Million." *International Herald Tribune*, Mar. 7–8, 1992, p. 11; Jackson, T. *Richard Branson, Virgin King: Inside Richard Branson's Business Empire.* Rocklin, Calif.: Prima, 1996; Kets de Vries, M., and Dick, R. "Richard Branson and the Virgin Group." INSEAD Case Study, 1989; Larson, E. "Then Came Branson." *Inc.*, Nov. 1987, p. 85; Parker-Pope, T. "When Richard Branson Considers the World, He Sees Lots and Lots of Virgin Territory." *Wall Street Journal Europe*, Oct. 14–15, 1994, p. 5; Sheff, D. "Richard Branson: The Interview." *Forbes*, Feb. 24, 1997, pp. 95–102; Usher, R. "Up, Up, and Away," *Time*, July 8, 1996, pp. 33–39.

2.   Branson, R. "Captain's Log: Branson Charts His Balloon Flight." *Times*, Jan. 13, 1997, p. 5.

Chapter Three

1.   Richard Branson was interviewed by author Kets de Vries.

PART TWO

Chapter Four

1.   Saito, and Maeda. "The Organizational Structure of One of the World's Most Powerful Companies." *Nikkei Business,* 1994, *1*(4), 19–22.

2.   Simons, R., and Barlett, C. "ASEA Brown Boveri." Case study no. 9-192-139. Cambridge, Mass.: Harvard Business School, 1992, p. 4.

3.   Wallace, C. "Percy Barnevik's Next Act." *Fortune*, May 26, 1997, p. 70.

Chapter Five

1.   Background research and interviews for this case study were done by Raafat Morcos, Christopher Grahn, Peter Gullander, and Casten von Otter.

2. Interview with Anders Vrethem, a subordinate of Barnevik's at Sandvik.

3. Taylor, W. "The Logic of Global Business: An Interview with ABB's Percy Barnevik." *Harvard Business Review,* Mar.–Apr., 1991, pp. 101, 104.

4. Interview with Frederik Bystrand, a subordinate of Barnevik's at Sandvik.

5. Florin, M., Frenkel, H., and Wilke, B. "Vi tvingades att bortse från alla lik i lasten." *Veckans Affärer,* Aug. 20, 1987, p. 62.

6. Arbose, J. "ABB: The New International Powerhouse." *International Management,* June 1988, *43*(6), 27.

7. Arbose (1988), p. 27.

8. Arbose (1988), p. 27.

9. Rapoport, C. "How Barnevik Makes ABB Work." *Fortune,* June 29, 1992, pp. 24–27.

10. Taylor (1991), p. 94.

11. Interview with Barnevik by author Kets de Vries.

12. Bartlett, C. A., and Ghoshal, S. "Beyond the M-Form: Toward a Managerial Theory of the Firm." *Strategic Management Journal,* Winter 1993, *14*, 23–46.

13. Taylor (1991), pp. 92–96.

14. Rapoport (1992), p. 27.

15. Interview with Leif Sunnermalm, a subordinate of Barnevik's at Sandvik; point confirmed in an interview with Bystrand.

16. Interview with Bennborn by Kets de Vries.

17. Interview with Olsson by Kets de Vries.

Chapter Six

1. Percy Barnevik was interviewed by Kets de Vries.

PART THREE

Chapter Seven

1. Sir Ronnie Hampel, chairman of ICI, quoted in the *Sunday Telegraph,* May 11, 1997, p. 16.

2. Buckley, N. "Scyther with a Softer Edge." *Financial Times,* Aug. 8–9, 1992, p. 18.

3. Dwyer, P. "So Far, What Simon Says Is Working at BP." *Business Week,* July 12, 1993, p. 21.

4. Kets de Vries, M.F.R., and Balazs, K. "Beyond the Quick Fix: The Psychodynamics of Organizational Transformation and Change." *INSEAD Working Paper* 97/113/ENT, 1997.

Chapter Eight

1. Lascelles, D., "Horton Is Ousted as Chairman of British Petroleum: Directors Point to Personality Clashes as Reason for Shock Decision." *Financial Times,* June 26, 1992, p. 19.

2. Harris, T., "BP USA: Horton's Tough Triumph." *Management Today,* May 1988, p. 47.

3. Lublin, J. "Who's News? Horton Seeks an American Accent for BP." *Wall Street Journal,* Feb. 14, 1989.

4. BP's *Annual Report 1988,* p. 2.

5. Cibin, R., and Grant, R. "Restructuring Among the World's Leading Oil Companies, 1980–1992." *British Journal of Management,* 1996, *7,* 303.

6. White, A. "Organizational Transformation at BP: An Interview with Chairman and CEO Robert Horton." *Human Resource Planning,* 1992, *15*(1), 13.

7. Hargreaves, I. "When Toughness Is Not Enough: The Background to the Resignation of Bob Horton, BP Chairman." *Financial Times,* June 26, 1992, p. 19.

8. White (1992), p. 12.

9. Mack, T. "Eager Lions and Reluctant Lions." *Forbes,* Feb. 17, 1992, p. 101.

10. "The Lessons of Mr Horton's Exit." *Financial Times,* June 29, 1992, p. 12.

11. "The Lessons . . ." (1992), p. 12.

12. Davidson, A. "David Simon." *Management Today,* July 1995, p. 50.

13. Bevan, J. "Simon: The Undaunted Optimist Uniting BP." *Sunday Telegraph,* Feb. 19, 1995, p. 3.

14. Connon, H. "They're All Doing What Simon Says." *Observer,* May 12, 1996, p. 8.

15. Connon (1996), p. 8.

16. Connon (1996), p. 8.

17. Anecdote told to author Kets de Vries by Sir David Simon.

18. Connon (1996), p. 7.

19. Bevan (1995), p. 3.

20. Lascelles (1992), p. 19.

21. All three are quoted in Davidson (1995), p. 50.

22. Hosking, P. "The Leader's Leader." *Independent on Sunday,* Dec. 31, 1995, p. B1.

23. "Management: Big Ideas and Big Books." *Financial Times,* Dec. 30, 1994, p. 14.

24. Bevan (1995), p. 3.

25. Hosking (1995), p. B1.

26. Mortished, C. "The Oilman Who Came in from the Cold." *London Times,* Nov. 23, 1996, p. 31.

27. Bahree, B. "BP Pulls Ahead of International Oil Peers; Cutting Costs, Using Better Technology Are Keys." *Wall Street Journal,* Sept. 8, 1995, p. 6.

28. Murray, S. "Well Ahead: BP's Hard Lesson: Downsizing Alone Won't Fix Problems." *Wall Street Journal Europe,* Sept. 16, 1997, p. 1.

29. Prokesch, S. "Unleashing the Power of Learning: An Interview with BP's John Browne." *Harvard Business Review,* Sept.–Oct., 1997, p. 160.

30. Browne, J. "Science, Technology, and Responsibility." Speech given to the Royal Society, London, Oct. 28, 1997.

31. Prokesch (1997), p. 153.

32. Prokesch (1997), p. 153.

33. Corzine, R. "People: John Browne, BP's Master of Recovery." *Financial Times,* Jan. 2, 1996, p. 8.

34. BP's *Annual Report and Accounts 1995,* p. 11.

35. Prokesch (1997), p. 155.

36. Prokesch (1997), p. 150.

37. Browne (1997).

38. Corzine, R. "John Browne Steps Up to Oil the Wheels at BP." *Financial Times,* July 3, 1995, p. 17.

39. BP's *Annual Report and Accounts 1995,* p. 4.

40. Glanville, B. "Influential Player Is Humble Fan." *Management Today,* Apr. 1996, p. 84.

41. Glanville (1996).

42. Dow Jones. "Company News: Europe Approves Oil Companies' Joint Operations." *New York Times,* Aug. 8, 1996, p. 4.

43. Corzine, R. "Companies and Finance: Europe's Savings from BP-Mobil Merger 'Higher Than Seen.'" *Financial Times,* Aug. 29, 1996, p. 23.

44. Brzezinski, M., and Bahree, B. "Pumped Up: Shell and BP Agree to Invest $1.75b in Russian Oil Firms." *Wall Street Journal Europe,* Nov. 18, 1997, pp. 1, 7.

45. Connon (1996), p. 8.

46. "Survey: Europe's Most Respected Companies, Europe's Top Managers." *Financial Times,* Sept. 18, 1996, p. 4.

47. "Observer: BP's Poetry in Motion." *Financial Times,* Aug. 9, 1995, p. 13.

Chapter Nine

1. Sir David Simon and John Browne were interviewed by author Kets de Vries.

Conclusion

1. ABB's *Annual Report*, 1994.
2. Interview with Richard Branson by author Kets de Vries.
3. "Management: Big Ideas . . ." (1994), p. 14.
4. Dullforce, W. "Where 'Paradise' Is to Be Found in Acting Quickly." *Financial Times*, Apr. 5, 1989, p. 18.
5. Kets de Vries, M.F.R., and Miller, D. *The Neurotic Organization*. San Francisco: Jossey-Bass, 1984.
6. Burger (1994), p. 33.
7. Ibrahim, Y. "BP's Browne: A Bit of Green in His Energy." *International Herald Tribune*, Dec. 13–14, 1997, p. 9.

About the Authors

Manfred F. R. Kets de Vries brings a fresh and unique view to the much-researched subject of leadership. Applying his eclectic training as an economist (Econ. Drs., University of Amsterdam), student of management (ITP, MBA, and DBA, Harvard Business School), and psychoanalyst (Canadian Psychoanalytic Society and the International Psychoanalytic Association), he probes the interface between international management, psychoanalysis, and dynamic psychiatry. His specific areas of interest are leadership, career dynamics, executive stress, entrepreneurship, family business, succession planning, cross-cultural management, and the dynamics of corporate transformation and change. He advises leaders on organizational design, strategic human resource management, and corporate transformation in leading U.S., Canadian, Pacific Rim, African, and European companies. He holds the Raoul de Vitry d'Avaucourt Chair of Human Resource Management at INSEAD, Fontainebleau, France. He is a clinical professor of management and leadership. He has held professorships at McGill University, the École des Hautes Études Commerciales (Montreal), and the Harvard Business School and has lectured at institutions around the world. He has five times received INSEAD's distinguished teacher award. He is a member of numerous editorial boards and a founding member of the International Society for the Psychoanalytic Study of Organizations. He is a regular columnist for a number of magazines. *The Financial Times, Le Capital, Wirtschaftswoche,* and the *Economist* have called Manfred Kets de Vries one of Europe's leading management thinkers.

Kets de Vries is the author or coauthor of more than 120 articles, has contributed chapters, and has produced numerous case studies (including some that were named the European Case Clearing House's best case of the year). He has written fourteen books, including *The Neurotic Organization: Diagnosing and Changing Counter-Productive Styles of Management* (1984, new edition 1990, with Danny Miller); *Organizations on the Couch* (1991); *Leaders, Fools, and Impostors* (1993); and the prize-winning *Life and Death in the Executive Fast Lane: Essays on Organizations and Leadership* (1995, Critics' Choice Award for 1995–96), all published by Jossey-Bass; *Power and the Corporate Mind* (1975, new edition 1985, with Abraham Zaleznik); *Organizational Paradoxes: Clinical Approaches to Management* (1980, new edition 1994); *The Irrational Executive: Psychoanalytic Explorations in Management* (1984, editor); *Unstable at the Top* (1988, with Danny Miller); *Prisoners of Leadership* (1989); *Handbook of Character Studies* (1991, with Sidney Perzow); *Family Business: Human Dilemmas in the Family Firm* (1996); and *Struggling with the Demon: Essays on Individual and Organizational Irrationality* (forthcoming). His books and articles have been translated into twelve languages. The Dutch government has made him an Officer in the Order of Oranje Nassau. He is the first fly fisherman to venture into Outer Mongolia with rod and reel and is a member of New York's Explorers Club.

Elizabeth Florent-Treacy is a research affiliate in management and leadership at INSEAD and a Ph.D. candidate in organization development at the Fielding Institute, Santa Barbara, California. Her work focuses on cross-cultural issues in global management and corporate transformation, as well as mergers and acquisitions. She studies not only the *how* of cross-cultural management but also the *why;* she is interested in looking beyond directly observable behavior. She has collaborated with Manfred Kets de Vries on many of his books and research projects, from works addressing family business and entrepreneurship to essays on the myth of the rational executive.

Index

Introduction

George Johansson, "Percy Barnevik's Recipe for Growth That Has Something for Everyone," *Dagens Industri/Europa,* Feb. 4, 1994, pp. 10–11. Used by permission of George Johansson.

Chapter One

From editorial "Republican Hot Air," *Daily Telegraph,* Jan. 8, 1997. Copyright © Telegraph Group Limited, London, 1997. Used by permission of the Telegraph Group Limited.

Chapter Five

Excerpts from "The Logic of Global Business: An Interview with ABB's Percy Barnevik," by William Taylor, *Harvard Business Review,* Mar.–Apr. 1991. Copyright © 1991 by the President and Fellows of Harvard College; all rights reserved. Reprinted by permission of *Harvard Business Review.*

Chapter Seven

Neil Buckley, "Scyther with a Softer Edge," *Financial Times,* Aug. 8–9, 1992, p. 18. Used by permission of the *Financial Times.*

Chapter Eight

J. Lublin, "Who's News? Horton Seeks an America Accent for BP," *Wall Street Journal,* Feb. 14, 1989. Reprinted by permission of *The Wall Street Journal,* copyright © 1989 Dow Jones & Company, Inc. All rights reserved worldwide.

Printed in the United Kingdom by
Lightning Source UK Ltd., Milton Keynes
138798UK00002BB/45/A

9 780787 946579